NEW EDITION

Grammar Essentials

Graded Exercises in English

ROBERT J. DIXSON

Longman

Grammar Essentials: Graded Exercises in English

Pearson Education, 10 Bank Street, White Plains, NY 10606

Acquisitions editor: Virginia L. Blanford
Development editor: Katherine Rawson
Production editor: Marc Oliver
Marketing manager: Joe Chapple
Senior manufacturing buyer: Nancy Flaggman
Cover and interior design: Tracey Munz Cataldo
Text composition: Carlisle Communications
Text font: Meta Plus Book 11/14

Library of Congress Cataloging-in-Publication Data

Dixson, Robert James.
    Grammar essentials : graded exercises in English / Robert J. Dixson—New ed.
        p. cm.
    New ed. of: Graded exercises in English. New ed. © 1994.
    ISBN 0-13-112696-2
    1. English language—Textbooks for foreign speakers. 2. English
language—Grammar—Problems, exercises, etc. I. Title.

PE1128.D5145 2004
428.2'4—dc22   2003060494

ISBN: 0-13-112696-2

LONGMAN ON THE WEB

Longman.com offers online resources for
teachers and students. Access our Companion
Websites, our online catalog, and our local
offices around the world.

Visit us at **longman.com**.

Printed in the United States of America
5 6 7 8 9 10 11 12–VHG–12 11 10 09 08

CONTENTS

The twenty-first century has brought a renewed emphasis on fundamentals in language learning. Mastery of basic grammar is once again seen as a critical building block of fluency. This workbook, first published almost thirty years ago, continues to provide the tools that students need to achieve grammar mastery.

Grammar Essentials, which was formerly published as *Graded Exercises in English,* is not designed to replace a regular classroom text. Rather, it is designed to supplement the text, to offer needed variety to a lesson, or simply to provide additional drill materials on important points of grammar and usage. Students will find it useful for self-study (an answer key is provided at the back) or for further practice on points about which they do not yet feel confident.

All explanatory material has been kept to a minimum. The grammar points that students need to know are presented in simple language, with clear examples, and students are then asked to complete exercises that provide practice in the correct use of those points. Many of these exercises will seem simple to a native speaker but provide real challenges to those studying English as a foreign or second language. This book is not designed to test knowledge. The exercises are not designed to find out how much a student knows or does not know. Their purpose is simply to provide practice (lots of practice!) on basic points of grammar and usage. These are *practice* exercises—nothing more. They provide an additional means for students to repeat materials that can be learned only through continuous use. For this reason, many exercises have been made as simple and clear as possible, and much direct repetition has been purposely introduced.

Grammar Essentials is organized in a step-by-step manner, from easier points to harder and more complex points. The structure echoes the standard sequence of an integrated or four-skills course.

This new edition retains its original features—over 100 grammar points presented, with over 2000 practice opportunities. Each page is tabbed, so topics can be easily found. New to this edition is a 16-page Quick Grammar Reference, which provides a fast, easy review of critical grammar points, including parts of speech, verb tenses, and an extensive list of irregular verbs.

The editors and publishers of Pearson Longman hope that this book will continue to provide help and encouragement to students of English, as Robert J. Dixson intended it to do when he first wrote it almost three decades ago.

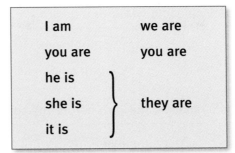

I am   we are

you are   you are

he is

she is   } they are

it is

Practice

Supply the correct form of the present tense of to be *as in the example.*

1. She ____is____ a good writer.

2. They _____ old friends.

3. I _____ a student.

4. John _____ absent from work today.

5. We _____ both students.

6. The weather today _____ good.

7. The sky _____ clear.

8. Henry and John _____ brothers.

9. She and I _____ cousins.

10. I _____ sick today.

11. She _____ a business person.

12. You _____ a lawyer.

13. Today _____ Wednesday.

14. She and José _____ both good writers.

15. The police officer on the corner _____ busy with the traffic.

16. You _____ old friends.

TO BE

Negatives and Questions

Form the negative of *to be* by placing *not* after the verb.

> I am an employee.
>
> I am *not* an employee.

Form questions with *to be* by placing the verb before the subject.

> They are absent from work today.
>
> *Are* they absent from work today?

Practice

A *Change the following sentences from affirmative to negative as in the example.*

1. She is in Japan now. *She is not in Japan now.* _____

2. You are angry. _____

3. Ben and Liz are cousins. _____

4. He is very serious. _____

5. Both sisters are tall. _____

6. She is a clever woman. _____

7. They are members of the country club. _____

8. He is a good tennis player. _____

9. Elaine is a pilot with an international airline. _____

10. The sky is very cloudy today. _____

11. The office of the supervisor is on the first floor. _____

12. It is cold today. _____

13. She is in her office. _____

14. The stamps are in my desk. _____

15. He is a smart man. _____

B *Change the sentences in Exercise A from statements to questions as in the example.*

She is in Japan now. *Is she in Japan now?* _____

A changes to *an* before any word beginning with a vowel sound.

a book	a man	a hotel
an apple	an orange	an hour
an old car	an early train	an ugly building
a useful tool	a one-page memo	a door

Practice

Complete the following sentences with a *or* an.

1. It is _____*a*_____ lovely day.

2. It is _____ old building.

3. He is _____ unusual man.

4. It is _____ exception to the rule.

5. It is _____ long trip, but it is _____ easy trip.

6. It is _____ large building.

7. He is _____ honest man.

8. She is _____ happy child.

9. The car is _____ used car.

10. It is _____ tall tree.

11. It is _____ egg.

12. It is _____ apple.

13. It is _____ old bus.

14. It is _____ empty milk carton.

15. It is _____ hour till lunch.

16. It is _____ windy day.

17. The gift is _____ new book.

18. It is _____ one-story building.

Most nouns form their plurals by adding *s*.

door ⟶ doors	doctor ⟶ doctors
pen ⟶ pens	apple ⟶ apples

Nouns ending in *s, z, ch, sh,* and *x* form their plurals by adding *es*.

box ⟶ boxes	class ⟶ classes
crash ⟶ crashes	church ⟶ churches

Some nouns have irregular plurals.

man ⟶ men	foot ⟶ feet	tooth ⟶ teeth
child ⟶ children	woman ⟶ women	mouse ⟶ mice

Practice

A *Give the plural forms of these nouns:*

friend	_friends_	dish	_____
salesman	_____	glass	_____
buzz	_____	player	_____
orange	_____	foot	_____

B *Change the following sentences from singular to plural as in the example.*

1. The pencil is on the desk. _The pencils are on the desk._

2. The glass is in the kitchen. _____

3. The dish is new. _____

4. The bus is at the corner. _____

5. The child is in the garden. _____

6. The clock is on the wall. _____

7. The watch is new. _____

8. The picture is beautiful. _____

Nouns that end in y form their plurals in one of two ways: if a vowel precedes the *y,* add *s*

| key → keys | toy → toys | tray → trays |

if a consonant precedes the *y,* change the *y* to *i* and add *es.*

| city → cities | lady → ladies | country → countries |

Most nouns that end in *f* or *fe* form their plurals by changing their endings to *ves.*

| wife → wives | leaf → leaves | half → halves |

Nouns that end in *o* and are preceded by a consonant form their plurals by adding *es.*

| hero → heroes | potato → potatoes |

Practice

Give the plural form of the noun in parentheses.

1. The (baby) need to take a nap. *The babies need to take a nap.*
2. The (knife) are in the drawer. _____
3. Those (tomato) aren't ripe. _____
4. The (boy) like to play soccer after school. _____
5. I keep my books on those (shelf). _____
6. You can see many (volcano) in Hawaii. _____
7. The (leaf) fall off the trees in the autumn. _____
8. They always put their (toy) in this box. _____
9. We like to eat (potato) with our dinner. _____
10. There are a lot of (thief) in this neighborhood. _____
11. The (key) are on the table. _____
12. I like to see the (butterfly) in my garden. _____

Present Tense

I have	we have
you have	you have
he has	
she has	they have
it has	

Practice

Complete the following sentences with the correct form of to have.

1. You ___*have*___ a new car.

2. She _____ one sister and two brothers.

3. You and I _____ many things in common.

4. Lou _____ a new wristwatch.

5. We _____ many friends in St. Louis.

6. Helen _____ a headache.

7. Grace _____ a date with George tonight.

8. They _____ a new telephone number.

9. Both brothers _____ red hair.

10. The dog _____ a long tail.

11. The office _____ three large windows.

12. I _____ an account at that bank.

13. Both children _____ bad colds.

14. Dr. Smith _____ many patients.

15. Ms. Jacobson, the lawyer, _____ many clients.

16. We _____ a large lunchroom at work.

17. The employee _____ a new computer.

18. The building _____ two entrances.

19. I _____ brown eyes.

20. You _____ green eyes.

The simple present tense describes an action which is a habit or a custom, or something that is always true.

I work	we work
you work	you work
he works	
she works	they work
it works	

Practice

Give the correct form of the present tense for the verb in parentheses.

1. She (read) the newspaper every day. _She reads the newspaper every day._
2. We (come) to work by bus. _____
3. I always (walk) to the office. _____
4. We (play) cards every afternoon. _____
5. I (eat) lunch in the cafeteria every day. _____
6. Helen (work) very hard. _____
7. I (like) to sit in the sun. _____
8. The dog (chase) the cat all around the house. _____
9. Mr. Smith (work) for a small airline. _____
10. Gene generally (sit) at this desk. _____
11. We always (play) tennis on Saturdays. _____
12. We always (cook) dinner at home. _____
13. They (eat) lunch together every day. _____
14. Many employees (ride) the bus to work. _____
15. They (take) a lot of trips together. _____
16. We always (travel) by car. _____
17. You (attend) class twice a week. _____
18. He (speak) several foreign languages. _____

SIMPLE PRESENT TENSE

Add *s* to most verbs to form the third person singular.
Add *es* when the verb ends in *o*

> go ⟶ goes   do ⟶ does

Add *es* when the verb ends in *sh, ch, s, x,* or *z*

> reach ⟶ reaches   wash ⟶ washes   fix ⟶ fixes

When a verb ends in a consonant plus *y,* change the *y* to *i* and add *es*

> study ⟶ studies   cry ⟶ cries   marry ⟶ marries

Practice

 A *Give the correct form of the present tense for the verb in parentheses.*

1. Pat (go) there twice a week. *Pat goes there twice a week.*

2. Herb (do) the work of two people. _____

3. I always (try) to arrive everywhere on time._____

4. George always (try) to do the same thing._____

5. The supervisor (wish) to speak with you. _____

6. Mr. Walker (teach) English and mathematics. _____

7. They (go) to the movies twice a week._____

8. We (watch) television almost every night._____

9. Mary (play) the piano very well. _____

10. He (study) in the same class as I._____

11. My father (watch) soccer on TV every weekend._____

12. Susan (kiss) her children good-bye every morning. _____

13. I often (catch) cold. _____

14. Helen also (catch) cold very often. _____

15. She (do) all the work. _____

16. She (carry) her papers in a briefcase. _____

B *Change the subject in each of the following sentences from* I *to* He. *Use the correct form of the verb.*

1. I like to read. _He likes to read._____
2. I teach science at a high school._____
3. I work hard._____
4. I own a car. _____
5. I live in Toronto. _____
6. I enjoy each English class._____
7. I want to learn French. _____
8. I have a new wristwatch. _____
9. I speak Spanish._____
10. I wish to learn English. _____
11. I read a book every night. _____
12. I pass Mr. Smith on the street every day._____
13. I always go to work by bus._____
14. I try to learn ten new words every day. _____
15. I do a lot of favors for Pauline. _____
16. I play the violin very well. _____
17. I have two brothers and two sisters. _____
18. I always sit at this desk. _____
19. I do my homework assignments in the evening. _____
20. I study English three times a week. _____

C *Change the subject of each sentence in Exercise B to* They. *Use the correct form of the verb.*

I like to read. _They like to read._____

D *Change the subject of each sentence in Exercise B to* She. *Use the correct form of the verb.*

I like to read. _She likes to read._____

my	our
your	your
his	
her	their
its	

I like *my* teacher.

She washes *her* car.

We eat *our* dinner at six o'clock.

They are in *their* classroom.

Practice

Complete the following sentences with the possessive adjective which refers to the subject of the sentence.

1. She knows ____*her*____ lesson well.

2. I also know _____ lesson well.

3. Gail likes _____ new job very much.

4. I feed _____ pets once a day.

5. You always get good grades on _____ examinations.

6. My daughters clean _____ room every Saturday.

7. Mr. Bach drives to work in _____ car.

8. Mary and I do _____ homework together.

9. Grace writes a letter to _____ aunt every week.

10. The dog wags _____ tail when it sees _____ dinner dish.

11. The children take _____ toys to the park.

12. I always write the new words in _____ notebook.

13. Each cat has _____ own dish for food and water.

14. Both boys ride _____ bicycles to work.

15. You and Henry spend a lot of time at _____ office.

16. We need to paint _____ house.

17. She always does well on all _____ examinations.

Affirmatives

We use *there is* with singular nouns; we use *there are* with plural nouns.

There is a book on the table.	**There are** books on the table.
There is one man in the room.	**There are** several men in the room.

Practice

Complete the following sentences with There is *or* There are.

1. *There are* no Australians in this class.
2. _____ someone at the door.
3. _____ a lot of students absent today.
4. _____ a mailbox on the corner.
5. _____ three lamps in the room.
6. _____ two large windows in the room.
7. _____ only one door.
8. _____ a lot of desks in our office.
9. _____ nobody in the room now.
10. _____ a letter on the table for you.
11. _____ several beautiful parks in this city.
12. _____ twelve months in a year.
13. _____ only one car in the parking lot.
14. _____ no one at home.
15. _____ dishes but no silverware on the table.
16. _____ no stores in this section of town.

THERE IS, THERE ARE

Negatives and Questions

The negative forms of *there is* and *there are* are formed by placing *not* after the verb. The contracted forms *isn't* and *aren't* are generally used.

There is a pencil in my bag.	There *isn't* a pencil in
There is *not* a pencil in my bag.	my bag.
There are two employees absent today.	There *aren't* two
There are *not* two employees absent today.	employees absent today.

The question forms of *there is* and *there are* are formed by placing the verb before *there*.

There is a window in the room.	There are four windows in the room.
Is there a window in the room?	*Are* there four windows in the room?

Practice

A *Change the following sentences from affirmative to negative. Use the contracted form.*

1. There is a flag at the top of the building. *There isn't a flag at the top of the building.*

2. There are two lamps in the room. _____

3. There is a pillow on each bed. _____

4. There are two police officers on each corner. _____

5. There is a big parade today. _____

6. There are many doctors in this area. _____

7. There are ten new words in this lesson. _____

8. There is a message for you on the hall table. _____

9. There are enough chairs for everyone. _____

10. There is a comfortable chair in each room. _____

11. There is a good restaurant near here. _____

12. There are telephones in every room. _____

B *Change the sentences in Exercise A to questions.*

There is a flag at the top of the building. 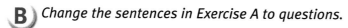 *Is there a flag at the top of the building?*

When a noun does not end in *s*, form the possessive by adding an apostrophe *s* (*'s*).

the boy ⟶ the *boy's* hat	the girl ⟶ the *girl's* ball
the lady ⟶ the *lady's* purse	the children ⟶ the *children's* games

When a noun already ends in *s*, form the singular possessive by adding an apostrophe *s* (*'s*) and form the plural possessive by adding only an apostrophe (*'*).

the boss ⟶ the *boss's* chair	the boys ⟶ the *boys'* hats
Charles ⟶ *Charles's* book	the ladies ⟶ the *ladies'* purses

Note that the possessive is used even when the noun modified is not expressed.

> She went to *Jonathan's*. (Jonathan's home)
>
> I have an appointment at the *doctor's*. (the doctor's office)

Practice

Insert the apostrophe in the correct places in the following sentences.

1. Mrs. Reagans car is outside. *Mrs. Reagan's car is outside.*
2. I left my books at Lauras house. _____
3. She buys her clothes in Chicagos best shops. _____
4. The mens room is just down the hall. _____
5. They sell ladies dresses on this floor. _____
6. The childs toys are all broken. _____
7. They sell childrens toys in this store. _____
8. There is a lot of competition between Bobs two sisters. _____
9. He goes to the doctors office once a week. _____
10. Lincolns Birthday is February 12. _____
11. Henry and Sallys father is in Europe. _____
12. Mrs. Jacksons daughter is eight years old. _____
13. St. Peters in Rome and St. Pauls in London are both good examples of Baroque architecture. _____

THIS/THAT; THESE/THOSE

This indicates that something is near us; *that* indicates that it is at a distance.

> **This** book is in my hand.
>
> **That** book is over there on the table.

The plural of *this* is *these;* the plural of *that* is *those.*

> **These** books are in my hand.
>
> **Those** books are over there on the table.

Practice

Change the following sentences from singular to plural.

1. This exercise is easy. *These exercises are easy.*_____

2. This room is too small for our furniture. _____

3. That pen on the floor is Sarah's. _____

4. This stack of CDs belongs to William. _____

5. That boy on the other side of the street is George's brother. _____

6. That book is out of date. _____

7. That purse on the table is Elizabeth's. _____

8. This is my chair. _____

9. That is Henry's pen. _____

10. This message is for you. _____

11. That letter on the table is for Ms. Thaler. _____

12. This is my pen, not Sandy's. _____

13. That mountain in the distance forms part of the Rocky Mountains. _____

14. This car belongs to my father. _____

15. That office at the end of the hall is the administration office. _____

16. This chair is very comfortable. _____

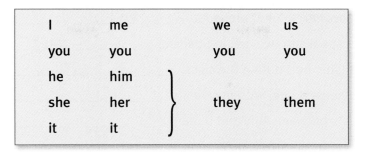

I	me	we	us
you	you	you	you
he	him		
she	her	they	them
it	it		

Object pronouns are used as direct objects, indirect objects, and objects of prepositions.

> She knows *me* well.
>
> We give *her* our homework every day.
>
> They give it to *us*.

Practice

 Choose the correct object pronoun form.

1. I often see (they, them) after work. *I often see them after work.* _____

2. She lives near (we, us). _____

3. We always go to lunch together with (she, her). _____

4. He teaches (we, us) English. _____

5. She sits near (I, me) during class. _____

6. I know both of (they, them) well. _____

7. I always speak to (he, him) in English. _____

8. What is the matter with (he, him) today? _____

9. He explains the lesson to (we, us) each morning. _____

10. There are some letters here for you and (I, me). _____

11. We want to divide the money between (we, us). _____

12. The Venezuelan lady knows (they, them) both well. _____

13. I know her sister and (she, her). _____

14. Mr. Johnson often helps Susan and (I, me). _____

15. He sends (she, her) a lot of presents. _____

16. She seldom speaks to (we, us) in Spanish. _____

17. He looks at (she, her) during the class. _____

18. She always helps (I, me) with my clients. _____

19. He always sits between Amy and (I, me). _____

20. He wants to talk with (they, them). _____

B *Substitute the correct object pronoun for the word or words in italics.*

1. I see *Mr. Park* during coffee break every morning. *I see him during coffee break every morning.*

2. I sit near *Grace and Frances* during the lesson. _____

3. All the boys like *Mary* very much. _____

4. I often see *you and your sister* at the supermarket. _____

5. He always goes to the movies with *his parents*. _____

6. I know *both boys* very well. _____

7. Frank always waits for *Al and me* after work. _____

8. He drives *Sue and Cal* to work every morning. _____

9. I sit next to *Carlos*. _____

10. I also sit directly in front of *Marsha*. _____

11. He writes a lot of letters to *his relatives*. _____

12. This book belongs to *William*. _____

13. I know *the dentist* very well. _____

14. The doctor relies on *her assistant*. _____

15. I understand *Miss McGrady*. _____

16. He always speaks to *his students* in English. _____

17. Everyone in our house plays cards except *my brother*. _____

18. He sends *his parents* money every week. _____

19. I talked to *Mr. and Mrs. Nelson* yesterday. _____

20. She saw *the women* after school. _____

The imperative form expresses a command or request. The subject *you* (singular or plural) is understood but not expressed.

Come back later.	**Wait outside.**

The negative of the imperative form uses *don't*.

Don't come back later.	**Don't wait outside.**

Please, used at the beginning or end of an imperative sentence, makes it more polite.

***Please* come back later.**	**Wait outside, *please*.**

Practice

 A *Give the imperative form of the following sentences.*

1. (Sit) there. *Sit there.* _____

2. (Give) this to Sally. _____

3. (Open) the door. _____

4. (Close) the door. _____

5. (Wait) in the outer office. _____

6. (Call) him in the morning. _____

7. (Let) him talk with her. _____

8. (Let) them talk. _____

9. (Turn) off the light. _____

10. (Put) your feet on the chair. _____

11. (Drop) this in the mailbox. _____

12. (Leave) your books there. _____

13. (Let) Alexandra know about this. _____

14. (Help) Jason with his homework. _____

15. (Send) money. _____

B *Give the negative imperative form of the sentences in Exercise A.*

(Sit) there. *Don't sit there.*

C *Make the sentences in Exercise A more polite by adding* please *at the beginning or end.*

(Sit) there. *Please sit there. Sit there, please.*

Negatives

Form the negative of the simple present tense by putting *do not* or *does not* before the verb. The contracted forms *don't* and *doesn't* are generally used.

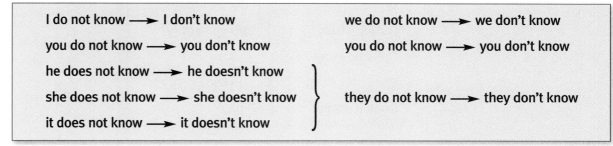

I do not know ⟶ I don't know   we do not know ⟶ we don't know

you do not know ⟶ you don't know   you do not know ⟶ you don't know

he does not know ⟶ he doesn't know

she does not know ⟶ she doesn't know   they do not know ⟶ they don't know

it does not know ⟶ it doesn't know

Note that after *does not (doesn't)*, the verb does not have the *s* of the third person singular affirmative statement.

Practice

Change the following sentences from affirmative to negative. Use both the full form and the contracted form.

1. I work on the tenth floor. *I do not work on the tenth floor. I don't work on the tenth floor.*

2. Ella likes to study English. _____

3. You speak English well. _____

4. The plane leaves at ten o'clock. _____

5. He knows everyone in the office. _____

6. I feel good. _____

7. He eats lunch in the cafeteria every day. _____

8. She always comes to work late. _____

9. They live in Chicago. _____

10. We need a fan in this room. _____

11. Janet and I cook together. _____

12. I understand everything he says. _____

13. She wants to visit San Francisco. _____

14. He begins his new job this week. _____

15. My son plays in the park every afternoon. _____

16. Gina and James make mistakes in spelling. _____

SIMPLE PRESENT TENSE

Yes-No Questions

Form *yes-no* questions in the simple present tense by placing *do* or *does* before the subject.

Do I study?	Do we study?
Do you study?	Do you study?
Does he study?	
Does she study?	Do they study?
Does it study?	

Note that after *does,* the verb does not have the third person singular *s.*

Practice

Change the following statements to questions as in the example.

1. Patricia goes to class twice a week. *Does Patricia go to class twice a week?*

2. They enjoy their cooking lessons. _____

3. That company buys a lot of merchandise from us. _____

4. It looks like rain. _____

5. He drives to Washington once a week. _____

6. The committee meets on the third floor. _____

7. He seems to be very busy. _____

8. This book belongs to her. _____

9. You like New York. _____

10. You speak French well. _____

11. He often goes out of town. _____

12. I take the Number 65 bus to my new job. _____

13. They sell newspapers there. _____

14. The store opens at nine o'clock. _____

15. It closes at five-thirty. _____

16. He eats a lot of vegetables. _____

Information Questions

Form information questions in the simple present tense by placing *do* or *does* before the subject and adding a question word.

> **Valerie lives in Vancouver.**
>
> **Where does Valerie live?**

Practice

 A *Supply* do *or* does *to complete these present tense questions.*

1. Where ___does___ Sam live?

2. How often _____ you go to the movies?

3. What time _____ the plane leave?

4. What language besides English _____ your teacher speak?

5. What time _____ you get up every morning?

6. What time _____ the rest of your family get up?

7. When _____ they get up every morning?

8. How well _____ Edna speak French?

9. Where _____ you usually meet Lois after the lesson?

10. How much _____ it cost to fly from Havana to Madrid?

11. How often _____ it rain during the month of April in your country?

12. How much _____ you generally pay for a pair of shoes?

13. How long _____ your meeting last?

14. What time _____ your meeting begin and what time does it end?

15. Where _____ you live?

16. How _____ you feel today?

17. Where _____ Ed go every day after work?

18. Where _____ you eat lunch every day?

Information Questions

19. What _____ you generally do over the weekend?

20. Which movie star _____ you like best?

21. Why _____ Jane want to study Russian?

22. How often _____ you go for a walk in the park?

B) *Change the following sentences to questions beginning with the question word in parentheses.*

1. They live in Boston. (Where) *Where do they live?* _____

2. The play begins at eight o'clock. (What time) _____

3. They get home at six o'clock every night. (When) _____

4. The travel agent speaks French poorly. (How well) _____

5. Those books cost $18.95. (How much) _____

6. They travel by car. (How) _____

7. He comes here once a week. (How often) _____

8. She feels good. (How) _____

9. Francine wants to learn English in order to get a better job. (Why) _____

10. They meet on the corner every morning. (Where) _____

11. We go to the movies twice a week. (How often) _____

12. The children go to the playground after lunch. (Where) _____

13. We learn ten new words everyday. (How many) _____

14. They eat lunch in the cafeteria. (Where) _____

15. He drives a small car. (What kind of car) _____

16. This plate belongs on the shelf. (Where) _____

17. The committee meets in Room 10. (Where) _____

18. She teaches us cooking. (What) _____

19. It rains in the spring. (When) _____

20. He gets up at seven o'clock every morning. (What time) _____

21. She goes to bed at ten o'clock. (When) _____

I was	we were
you were	you were
he was	
she was	they were
it was	

Practice

Supply the correct form of the past tense of to be *as in the example.*

1. Teresa _____was_____ absent from work yesterday.

2. He _____ in the same office as Wendy last year.

3. They _____ in the same class last semester.

4. The office door _____ open this morning.

5. But both windows _____ closed.

6. Ned _____ not at work yesterday.

7. He and his sister _____ sick.

8. You _____ busy all day yesterday.

9. We _____ tired after our long walk.

10. I _____ hungry after so much exercise.

11. There _____ a lot of members absent from the meeting yesterday.

12. Fred _____ present, but I _____ not.

13. The weather yesterday _____ very warm.

14. We _____ pleased to receive your memorandum.

15. You _____ not satisfied with my memorandum.

16. The exercises in the last lesson _____ easy.

17. We _____ not able to get in touch with Mr. Reese yesterday.

18. The wind last night _____ very strong.

TO BE

Past Tense Negatives and Questions

Form the negative of the past tense of *to be* by placing *not* after the verb. The contracted forms *wasn't* and *weren't* are generally used.

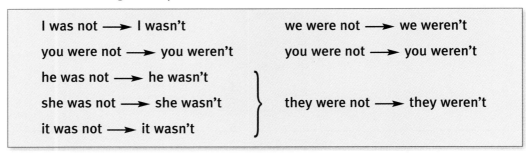

I was not ⟶ I wasn't

you were not ⟶ you weren't

he was not ⟶ he wasn't

she was not ⟶ she wasn't

it was not ⟶ it wasn't

we were not ⟶ we weren't

you were not ⟶ you weren't

they were not ⟶ they weren't

Form questions in the past tense of *to be* by placing the verb before the subject.

They were here yesterday.	Were they here yesterday?

Practice

 A *Change the following sentences from affirmative to negative. Use both the full form and the contracted form.*

1. You were tired last night. *You were not tired last night. You weren't tired last night.*

2. These doors were closed. _____

3. The exercises were easy to do. _____

4. The man was a stranger to her. _____

5. It was a pleasant day. _____

6. The sea was very rough. _____

7. He was a tall man. _____

8. There were ten new words in the lesson. _____

9. Sarah was a good swimmer. _____

10. She was very intelligent. _____

11. They were both Americans. _____

12. She was a good tennis player. _____

13. You were a happy child. _____

14. He was always angry. _____

24 Grammar Essentials

Past Tense Negatives and Questions

15. They were friendly enemies. _____

16. Bert was an old friend of the family. _____

B *Change the sentences in Exercise A to questions.*

You were tired last night. *Were you tired last night?* _____

Regular Verbs

Form the past tense of regular verbs by adding *ed* to their simple form.

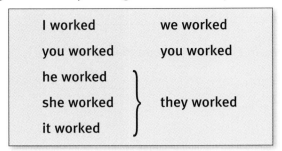

I worked	we worked
you worked	you worked
he worked	
she worked	they worked
it worked	

Note these spellings:

live ⟶ lived   study ⟶ studied

Practice

Supply the past tense form of the verbs in parentheses.

1. We (work) in our garden all day yesterday. *We worked in our garden all day yesterday.*

2. I (listen) to the stereo until twelve o'clock last night. _____

3. Meg and I (talk) on the telephone yesterday. _____

4. He always (want) to learn English. _____

5. They (live) in France for many years. _____

6. We (expect) to go to China in June. _____

7. The meeting (last) about two hours. _____

8. We (change) planes in Seattle. _____

9. We both (like) the movies last night very much. _____

10. I (wait) almost two hours for Gertrude. _____

11. They (paint) their house white. _____

12. She (arrive) late to the meeting. _____

13. We (watch) television until eleven o'clock last night. _____

14. She (study) in our class last semester. _____

15. I (mail) your letter on my way to work. _____

Irregular Verbs

Irregular verbs, like regular verbs, have the same form in all persons of the past tense.

I ate	we ate
you ate	you ate
he ate, she ate, it ate	they ate

Practice

 A *Memorize and practice the past tense forms of these irregular verbs:*

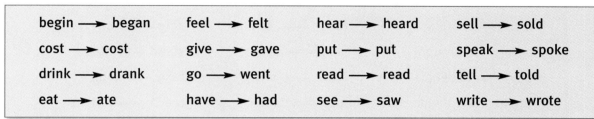

begin → began	feel → felt	hear → heard	sell → sold
cost → cost	give → gave	put → put	speak → spoke
drink → drank	go → went	read → read	tell → told
eat → ate	have → had	see → saw	write → wrote

B *Supply the past tense form of the verbs in parentheses.*

1. Mr. and Mrs. Rockwell (come) to visit us last night. *Mr. and Mrs. Rockwell came to* _____ *visit us last night.* _____

2. They (tell) us about their plans for their new home. _____

3. The weather was warm, so we (sit) on our front porch. _____

4. I (put) your coat in the closet. _____

5. The meeting last night (begin) at eight and ended at ten. _____

6. I stayed home last night and (write) several letters. _____

7. I (see) you on the street yesterday. _____

8. This book (cost) $15.50. _____

9. I (eat) my lunch in the cafeteria yesterday. _____

10. Bob (drink) a little wine at the party last night. _____

11. I (give) your message and also (tell) him my ideas on the subject. _____

12. Ms. Sato finally (sell) her house. _____

13. I (hear) the President speak on television last night. _____

PAST TENSE

Irregular Verbs

14. My father (know) Mr. Evans well even before he (come) to live in this town. _____

15. Kim (feel) well yesterday, but today she feels sick again. _____

16. We (go) to the park yesterday and I (get) wet when it rained. _____

17. I (read) the novel several years ago. _____

18. You (have) a cold last week. _____

19. Senator Jordan (speak) to our club last month. _____

C *Memorize and practice the past tense forms of these irregular verbs:*

become → became	find → found	send → sent
break → broke	forget → forgot	sing → sang
bring → brought	keep → kept	stand → stood
buy → bought	leave → left	take → took
catch → caught	lose → lost	teach → taught
do → did	make → made	think → thought
fight → fought	ring → rang	understand → understood

D *Supply the correct past tense form of the verbs in parentheses.*

1. The plane (leave) Buenos Aires last night at midnight. *The plane left Buenos Aires last night at midnight.*

2. Sue (bring) her cousin to the party last night. _____

3. I (forget) to bring my notes to the meeting this morning. _____

4. He (become) president of the company five years ago. _____

5. We (make) good time on our trip from Houston to Mexico City. _____

6. I (lose) my book yesterday but (find) it later. _____

7. The two men (fight) bitterly over the division of the money. _____

8. The telephone (ring) twice, but no one answered it. _____

9. The Kanes (send) their three children to summer camp. _____

10. George (think) about his troubles continuously. _____

11. Last year Professor Levy (teach) us both English and mathematics. _____

12. They (buy) the property in 1990 and (sell) it in 2003. _____

13. Carl (keep) part of the money and (give) the rest to his two brothers. _____

14. The police (do) their best but never (catch) the real bank robbers. _____

15. The woman (sing) in French; consequently, we (understand) none of the words. _____

16. We (stand) on the corner and waited for Mel for two hours. _____

17. I (break) my stereo, so yesterday I (take) it to the repair shop. _____

E *Memorize and practice the past tense forms of these irregular verbs:*

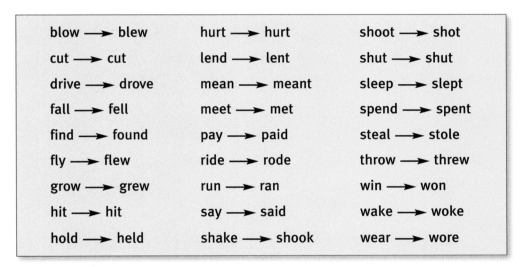

blow → blew	hurt → hurt	shoot → shot
cut → cut	lend → lent	shut → shut
drive → drove	mean → meant	sleep → slept
fall → fell	meet → met	spend → spent
find → found	pay → paid	steal → stole
fly → flew	ride → rode	throw → threw
grow → grew	run → ran	win → won
hit → hit	say → said	wake → woke
hold → held	shake → shook	wear → wore

F *Complete the following sentences with the past tense form of the irregular verbs in parentheses.*

1. Charles _____fell_____ (fall) from his bike and hurt his arm.

2. I _____ (pay) sixteen dollars for this book.

3. We _____ (shake) hands and then _____ (say) good night.

4. The force of the wind was so great that it _____ (blow) down several trees in our yard.

5. The pitcher _____ (throw) a slow ball and the batter _____ (hit) it for a home run.

6. I _____ (sleep) very well last night.

7. We _____ (meet) Ivy on the corner of Oak Avenue.

8. She finally _____ (find) her lost book.

Irregular Verbs

9. Alma _____ (wear) her new silk dress to the party last night.

10. The drunken driver first _____ (cut) in front of us and then _____ (run) his car over the curb.

11. We _____ (drive) to Washington in Noel's new car.

12. He _____ (hold) the bird in his hand for several minutes.

14. Our team _____ (win) the first game but _____ (lose) the second.

15. We _____ (shut) all the windows and locked all the doors before we _____ (go) out.

16. We rented two horses and _____ (ride) all around the park on horseback.

Negatives

Form past tense negatives by placing *did not* before the verb and by changing the verb to its simple form. The contracted form *didn't* is generally used.

I *went.*	I *did not* go.	I *didn't* go.

I did not go ⟶ I didn't go   we did not go ⟶ we didn't go

you did not go ⟶ you didn't go   you did not go ⟶ you didn't go

he did not go ⟶ he didn't go

she did not go ⟶ she didn't go   they did not go ⟶ they didn't go

it did not go ⟶ it didn't go

Practice

Change the following sentences from affirmative to negative. Use both the full form and the contracted form.

1. They ate chicken for dinner. *They did not eat chicken for dinner.*
   They didn't eat chicken for dinner.

2. You told me about it. _____

3. He put the books on the table. _____

4. They stayed in Mexico City. _____

5. Judy and I saw Eliot yesterday. _____

6. He planned his work well. _____

7. The meeting lasted a long time. _____

8. The book cost $13.95. _____

9. Gina and her husband worked together. _____

10. I knew him very well. _____

11. They sold their home. _____

12. I spoke with George about that matter. _____

13. She came to the meeting alone. _____

14. We sat together at the concert last night. _____

15. I went to Bermuda by boat. _____

16. You gave her your message. _____

Yes-No Questions

Form past tense questions by placing *did* before the subject and by changing the verb to its simple form.

She went home.	*Did* she go home?
Did I work?	Did we work?
Did you work?	Did you work?
Did he work?	
Did she work?	Did they work ?
Did they work?	

Practice

Change the following past tense statements to questions as in the example.

1. She lived in Peru for two years. _Did she live in Peru for two years?_

2. He gave her a lot of presents. _____

3. They stayed in Korea all summer. _____

4. She told them all about her trip. _____

5. You moved here in February. _____

6. Terry flew to Minneapolis. _____

7. We went home late last night. _____

8. They came to the party together. _____

9. Carla and Dave knew each other as children. _____

10. He worked in that firm for many years. _____

11. She felt much better after her operation. _____

12. The meeting began on time. _____

13. I passed all my examinations. _____

14. They put him in the advanced class. _____

15. I gave you my cell phone number. _____

16. The crowd waited a long time to see the President. _____

Information Questions

Form information questions in the past tense by placing *did* before the subject, changing the verb to its simple form, and adding a question word.

> **She went home at 9:30.**
>
> **What time did she go home?**

Practice

Change the following past tense statements to questions beginning with the question word in parentheses.

1. Marianne arrived at ten o'clock. (What time) *What time did Marianne arrive?*

2. They sold their home last week. (When) _____

3. The meeting began at eight-thirty. (What time) _____

4. The tickets cost three dollars. (How much) _____

5. He paid for the car by check. (How) _____

6. She invested ten thousand dollars in the stock market. (How much) _____

7. They sat in the first row. (Where) _____

8. He spoke to them last night. (When) _____

9. The meeting lasted two hours. (How long) _____

10. It began at eight o'clock. (What time) _____

11. I called her at two o'clock. (What time) _____

12. He went to Denver to see some friends. (Why) _____

13. You mentioned it to him three or four times. (How many times) _____

14. They ate lunch in the park. (Where) _____

15. We worked there for five years. (How many years) _____

16. I put the mail on Mr. Agee's desk. (Where) _____

17. She waited for them for an hour. (How long) _____

18. We got home around midnight. (What time) _____

19. He walked to the meeting with Peg. (Who) _____

20. You went to the park after the lesson. (Where) _____

Negatives and Questions

Practice

A *Change the following sentences from affirmative to negative.*

1. They live in Texas. *They do not live in Texas. They don't live in Texas.*

2. There are eleven months in a year. _____

3. The plane arrived at ten o'clock. _____

4. It is six o'clock now. _____

5. He went to Chicago by plane. _____

6. The two boys are in Ms. Collier's office. _____

7. The magazine cost two dollars. _____

8. They live in Sao Paulo now. _____

9. They lived in France for ten years. _____

10. He got up at five o'clock this morning. _____

11. They sat in the park for two hours. _____

12. She speaks English. _____

13. The meeting begins at nine o'clock. _____

14. She drinks ten cups of coffee every day. _____

15. They began to work in June. _____

16. I am ten years old. _____

17. They plan to finish the work in July. _____

18. We got sick last week. _____

19. The stores were closed because of the holiday. _____

B *Change the sentences in Exercise A to questions.*

They live in Texas. *Do they live in Texas?*

C *Change the sentences in Exercise A to questions beginning with a question word.*

They live in Texas. *Where do they live? Why do they live in Texas?*

Regular and Irregular Verbs

The past tense form of regular verbs adds *ed* to the simple form.

work ⟶ worked   study ⟶ studied   cry ⟶ cried

The past tense form of irregular verbs must be memorized.

tell ⟶ told   go ⟶ went   see ⟶ saw

Practice

Complete the following sentences with the past tense form of the verbs in parentheses.

1. The police __caught__ (catch) the thief after the robbery.

2. The students _____ (write) the sentences on the blackboard.

3. Edgar _____ (forget) to bring his notes to the meeting.

4. The plane _____ (arrive) an hour late.

5. Gwen _____ (answer) all the doctor's questions.

6. The secretary _____ (make) some mistakes in the letter.

7. The bell _____ (ring) ten minutes ago.

8. I _____ (wait) for Beth for half an hour.

9. The students _____ (go) to class when the bell _____ (ring).

10. Our new car _____ (cost) more than twenty thousand dollars.

11. I _____ (try) to get to work on time yesterday.

12. He _____ (have) a very good time at the picnic.

13. They _____ (plan) to take their vacation in June.

14. Al _____ (take) his vacation in May last year.

15. Amos _____ (send) a present to his mother.

16. Joyce _____ (need) a new umbrella for months; she finally _____ (buy) one last week.

17. The teacher _____ (speak) to the students' parents.

18. He _____ (tell) them that they _____ (have) to study harder.

19. You _____ (break) a lot of dishes last week.

Position

If the indirect object follows the direct object, we use the preposition *to* or *for*. If the indirect object precedes the direct object, we do not use a preposition.

He gave the money *to me*.	He gave *me* the money.
I bought a present *for you*.	I bought *you* a present.

Practice

A *Restate the following, putting the indirect object before the direct object.*

1. He sent several letters to her. *He sent her several letters.*

2. She brought the magazines *to me*. _____

3. She sent flowers *to them*. _____

4. He told the whole story *to us*. _____

5. I cooked dinner *for Victoria*. _____

6. We wrote several letters *to them*. _____

7. I took the presents *to her*. _____

8. He sold his property *to a friend*. _____

9. He gave a piece of the candy *to each child*. _____

10. Don't show these pictures *to anyone*. _____

11. He bought several new dresses *for his wife*. _____

12. They sent some postcards *to us* from South America. _____

B *Restate the following, putting the indirect object after the direct object.*

1. She gave me the money. *She gave the money to me.*

2. I sent *her* many presents. _____

3. Please hand *me* that magazine. _____

4. Don't tell *her* the news yet. _____

5. You made *your sister* a sweater. _____

6. Don't show *Flo* these things. _____

Position

7. He wrote *me* a letter on Wednesday. _____

8. She told *us* the whole story. _____

9. The teacher gives *us* a lot of homework. _____

10. You made *me* a promise that you must keep. _____

Who/Whom, Which, and That

Who refers to people. *Which* refers to specific animals or things. *That* refers to animals, things, or people as a class. The object (direct or indirect) form of *who* is *whom*. *Which* and *that* both have the same form whether subject or object.

> The man *who* called you is here.
>
> The girl *whom* you saw is my sister.
>
> To *whom* did you give the key?
>
> Is this the book *which* you ordered?
>
> The magazine *which* is on the table is old.
>
> The Native Americans *that* lived here were called Sioux.
>
> These are the colors *that* we like.

Practice

Complete the following sentences with who, whom, which, *or* that.

1. Was it Jennifer ___who___ said that?

2. This is the report _____ the president wanted.

3. The girls _____ are in my class are all good students.

4. Our teacher, _____ is an American, speaks English perfectly.

5. The car _____ Hernando used belongs to his uncle.

6. The teacher with _____ I studied mathematics last year died last week.

7. To _____ did you sell your furniture?

8. Is this the program _____ you always watch on TV?

9. The movies _____ we saw this summer were all good.

10. These are the kinds of exercises _____ help us learn English.

11. The lamp _____ you broke is my brother's.

12. She is one of the workers _____ went on strike.

13. She was the pilot _____ flew our 747.

14. It is the little things in life _____ count.

The future is expressed with *will* and the simple form of the verb. The contracted forms are generally used.

I will go → I'll go		we will go → we'll go	
you will go → you'll go		you will go → you'll go	
he will go → he'll go			
she will go → she'll go		they will go → they'll go	
it will go → it'll go			

Practice

Complete the following sentences with will *and the verbs in parentheses. Use both the full form and the contracted form.*

1. He __will call__ (call) you tomorrow. *He'll call you tomorrow.* _____

2. They _____ (see) us in the morning. _____

3. They _____ (be) happy to see you. _____

4. She _____ (help) you with that work. _____

5. Mary _____ (clean) off the table right away. _____

6. The stores _____ (close) early today. _____

7. I _____ (leave) the tip. _____

8. Helen _____ (find) the book that you need. _____

9. You _____ (spend) a lot of money there. _____

10. Ms. Koboski _____ (be) in New Orleans. _____

11. The wind _____ (blow) that sign down. _____

12. We _____ (meet) you in Grand Central Station. _____

13. I _____ (pay) the bill. _____

14. You _____ (learn) a great deal in that course. _____

15. We _____ (remain) in Tokyo about a month. _____

16. We _____ (be) tired after the long drive. _____

17. I _____ (give) you that money tomorrow. _____

18. John _____ (do) well in that job. _____

Negatives with *Will*

Place *not* after *will* to form a negative statement. The contracted form of *will not* is *won't*.

I will not stop ⟶ I won't stop   we will not stop ⟶ we won't stop

you will not stop ⟶ you won't stop   you will not stop ⟶ you won't stop

he will not stop ⟶ he won't stop

she will not stop ⟶ she won't stop   they will not stop ⟶ they won't stop

it will not stop ⟶ it won't stop

Practice

Change the following sentences from affirmative to negative. Use both the full form and the contracted form.

1. They will arrive on time. _They will not arrive on time. They won't arrive on time._

2. We will tell Tim about it. _____

3. I will be back in an hour. _____

4. The weather will be cool tomorrow. _____

5. He will be able to meet us later. _____

6. These exercises will be easy for you. _____

7. We will eat in the same restaurant again. _____

8. You will get tired of that work. _____

9. We will be there before Wednesday. _____

10. I will do well in that job. _____

11. They will sign the contract tomorrow. _____

12. They will finish the work in April. _____

13. The meeting will last an hour. _____

14. The stores will close at noon today. _____

15. It will cost a lot of money to remodel that house. _____

16. We will be ready to leave in an hour. _____

Place *will* before the subject to form yes-no questions.

Will I go?	Will we go?
Will you go?	Will you go?
Will he go?	
Will she go?	Will they go?
Will it go?	

Add a question word to form an information question.

Where will they go?	When will they go?	Why will they go?

Practice

A *Change the following sentences to questions.*

1. They'll arrive on Wednesday. *Will they arrive on Wednesday?*

2. I'll be back at three o'clock. _____

3. The stores will be open until six o'clock. _____

4. It'll cost $200 to fix the computer. _____

5. The plant will die because of lack of sunlight. _____

6. They'll spend two months in France. _____

7. She'll meet us in the supermarket. _____

8. They'll pay their bill next week. _____

9. The meeting will begin at eight o'clock. _____

10. It'll last an hour. _____

11. She'll leave a message on the table for him. _____

12. You'll return in October. _____

13. There will be three new members in the club. _____

14. The meeting will be over at three o'clock. _____

15. They'll write to us on Wednesday. _____

B *Change the sentences in Exercise A to questions beginning with question words.*

They'll arrive on Wednesday. *When will they arrive?* _____

Use infinitives to complete the meaning of various verbs.

> **He wants *to see you*.**
>
> **We tried *to call you*.**

Use infinitives to complete the meaning of various adjectives and adverbs.

> **These exercises are easy *to do*.**
>
> **It was impossible *to open* that door.**

Use infinitives either alone or after *in order* to express the idea of purpose.

> **He went there *to see* his friend.**
>
> **We came early *in order to get* good seats.**

Practice

Using infinitive constructions, complete the following sentences in your own words.

1. I'll be glad <u>to help you with your homework</u>.
2. He went here in order _____.
3. She wants _____.
4. I prefer _____.
5. It is easy _____.
6. We hope _____.
7. They are afraid _____.
8. You went there _____.
9. You went there in order _____.
10. I forgot _____.
11. It was impossible _____.
12. We both like _____.
13. You need _____.
14. I told him _____.
15. You don't want _____.
16. It is hard _____.
17. They expect _____.
18. It is possible _____.
19. We are too weak _____.
20. I know how _____.
21. Did you forget _____?

It takes expresses a period of time which is necessary in order to complete some action. *It takes* is always followed by an infinitive.

> ***It takes me*** forty-five minutes to get ready in the morning. (Present)
>
> ***It took us*** three weeks to finish the project. (Past)
>
> ***It will (It'll) take*** you a half-hour to change that tire. (Future)

Practice

Change each of the following sentences so that it begins with a present tense, past tense, or future tense form of it takes *as required by the meaning.*

1. She walked to work in ten minutes. *It took her ten minutes to walk to work.*

2. I finished my work in an hour. _____

3. She learned to speak English well in only one year. _____

4. I wrote my paper in thirty minutes. _____

5. The train went around the mountain in three hours. _____

6. They finished the bridge in one year. _____

7. The package reached him in two days. _____

8. We walk to school every morning in about fifteen minutes. _____

9. You'll get there in about an hour. _____

10. We'll paint the bathroom in two hours. _____

11. You'll paint the kitchen in only one and one-half hours. _____

12. I wash and dress each morning in less than fifteen minutes. _____

13. The clown puts on his makeup in half an hour. _____

14. He learned to swim in just a few days. _____

15. She recovered from her illness in two months. _____

16. I'll run to the corner store and get what you need in just two or three minutes. _____
_____

PRESENT CONTINUOUS TENSE

Form the present continuous tense by placing the appropriate form of *to be* before the present participle (*ing* form) of the main verb. The contracted forms are generally used.

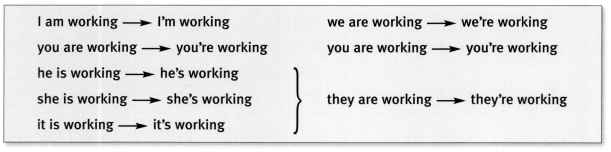

The present continuous tense describes an action that is going on at the present moment.

> He *is talking* with her now.   It's *raining*.

Practice

Complete the following sentences with the present continuous tense form of the verbs in parentheses.

1. They __are waiting__ (wait) for us on the corner now.

2. The bus _____ (stop) for us now.

3. Listen! I think the telephone _____ (ring).

4. I see that you _____ (wear) your new suit today.

5. Look! It _____ (begin) to rain.

6. Listen! Someone _____ (knock) at the door.

7. Please be quiet! The baby _____ (sleep).

8. Look! The cat _____ (try) to climb that tall tree.

9. Janet _____ (do) well in her studies.

10. The leaves _____ (begin) to fall from the trees.

11. John _____ (have) lunch in the cafeteria now.

12. Listen! That's Eve who _____ (play) the piano.

13. At present they _____ (travel) in South America.

14. For the time being, Mr. Collins _____ (act) as manager of this department.

15. All the big stores _____ (have) sales this month.

Note the difference between the simple present tense and the present continuous tense. The present tense describes actions that occur every day or all the time, while the present continuous tense describes actions that are happening now.

Peter talks to Anne all the time.	(Present)
Peter is talking to Anne at this moment.	(Present Continuous)

Practice

Supply the simple present tense or the present continuous tense as required by the meaning of the sentence.

1. Mr. Hansen often ____*travels*____ (travel) to Atlanta on business.

2. Our club _____ (meet) two times every week.

3. Mr. Cole _____ (teach) us at present. He _____ (substitute) for Mr. Russell, who is our regular teacher.

4. Every hour our churchbell _____ (ring). Listen! I believe it _____ (ring) now.

5. Stella _____ (watch) TV now. I believe that she always _____ (watch) a show at this time.

6. Listen! Someone _____ (knock) at the door.

7. Jay never _____ (come) to work on time.

8. At this moment I _____ (read) sentence number 8 in the exercise.

9. The wind always _____ (blow) hard in this section of town.

10. For the time being, while Mr. Press is away, Ms. Brennan _____ (acts) as manager of our department.

11. This store _____ (have) a big sale on shoes today.

12. Kurt seems to be very busy. I guess he _____ (study) for his science test.

13. I _____ (get) up at seven o'clock every morning.

14. Ed usually _____ (stay) in a hotel when he _____ (come) to town, but tonight he _____ (stay) with us.

15. The sun always _____ (rise) in the east. Look! It _____ (rise) now.

16. Mr. and Mrs. Bush _____ (build) a new home on Hollywood Boulevard.

PRESENT CONTINUOUS TENSE

Negatives and Questions

Form present continuous tense negatives by placing *not* after the auxiliary *to be*. The contracted forms are generally used.

> **She is studying English.**
>
> **She is** *not* **studying English.**   **She** *isn't* **studying English.**

Form present continuous tense questions by placing the *to be* auxiliary before the subject.

> **They are working.**   *Are* **they working?**

Practice

 A *Change the following sentences from affirmative to negative.*

1. The telephone is ringing. <u>*The telephone is not ringing. The telephone isn't ringing.*</u>

2. It is beginning to rain. _____

3. The sky is getting very dark. _____

4. She is working on the fourth floor at present._____

5. The maid is cleaning the room now._____

6. They are taking a walk in the park._____

7. You are having lunch outside._____

8. John is doing well in his studies at present. _____

9. We are laughing at what you said. _____

10. They are traveling in Europe at present. _____

11. I am taking dancing lessons._____

12. The leaves are beginning to fall from the trees. _____

13. All the birds are flying south. _____

14. Ellen is writing a series of articles on the economic situation. _____

B *Change the sentences from Exercise A to questions.*

The telephone is ringing. <u>*Is the telephone ringing?*</u>

Affirmative

These contracted forms are used more frequently than their full forms in spoken English.

I am ⟶ I'm	I will ⟶ I'll
You are ⟶ You're	You will ⟶ You'll
He/She/It is ⟶ He's/She's/It's	He/She/It will ⟶ He'll/She'll/It'll
We are ⟶ We're	We will ⟶ We'll
They are ⟶ They're	They will ⟶ They'll

Note that the following types of contractions with objects or proper nouns as subjects of the sentence appear in spoken English but generally not in written English.

The telephone is ringing.	The telephone's ringing.
The Reagans are on vacation.	The Reagans're on vacation.

Practice

Give the contracted forms of the verbs in these sentences.

1. She is a good employee. *She's a good employee.*

2. They are waiting for us on the tenth floor. _____

3. I will be back before noon. _____

4. She is very busy. _____

5. It is raining hard. _____

6. She will surely finish the work today. _____

7. We are old friends. _____

8. They are planning to leave next week. _____

9. It is almost three o'clock. _____

10. We are coming next Friday. _____

11. You will lose my keys if you play with them. _____

12. It is just leaving the station now. _____

13. There is someone at the door. _____

14. They will remain in Japan all summer. _____

Negative

These contracted forms are used more frequently than their full forms in spoken English.

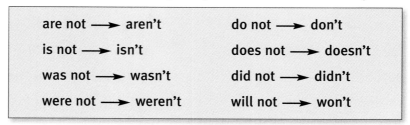

are not ⟶ aren't   do not ⟶ don't

is not ⟶ isn't   does not ⟶ doesn't

was not ⟶ wasn't   did not ⟶ didn't

were not ⟶ weren't   will not ⟶ won't

Practice

Use the contracted forms of these negative verbs.

1. He did not come to the meeting yesterday. *He didn't come to the meeting yesterday.*

2. They do not speak English well. _____

3. She is not studying science at present. _____

4. He is not a good manager. _____

5. They are not satisfied with their new apartment. _____

6. He does not appreciate your help. _____

7. You did not talk to the manager. _____

8. She does not spend much money on entertainment. _____

9. You are not the only person who feels that way about Melissa. _____

10. We were not pleased with the results of our examinations. _____

11. George was not at the meeting last night. _____

12. She and her husband do not get along well. _____

13. I will not be back before six. _____

14. There were not many employees absent from work today. _____

15. They will not leave for Paris before next month. _____

16. You are not doing that exercise correctly. _____

17. There are not any good shows on television tonight. _____

Indefinite and Definite

A and *an* are indefinite articles. They refer to objects that have not been specifically identified.

> **A book is on the table.**

The indefinite article (*a* or *an*) is used only with singular nouns.

> **There is a *book* on the table.**   **There are *books* on the table.**

The is a definite article. It refers to a particular object.

> **The book that I am reading is on the table.**

The definite article *(the)* is used with both singular and plural nouns.

> **The *book* that I am reading is on the table.**
> **The *books* that I am reading are on the table.**

The is also used with definite noncountable nouns (nouns that don't usually have a plural form).

> **The *gold* in this ring is very old.**

Indefinite noncountable nouns don't take an article.

> **Gold is an important metal.**

Practice

Complete the following sentences with the correct article.

1. ___The___ chair you are sitting in is very comfortable.
2. There is _____ pencil (no particular pencil) on the desk.
3. There is _____ customer (no particular customer) outside who wishes to see Mrs. Winston.
4. _____ customer whom Mr. Garp telephoned this morning is here now.
5. I want to find _____ good book (no particular book) to read tonight.
6. _____ book which I am reading now belongs to Leslie.
7. _____ book which gave me the greatest pleasure was *Les Misérables*.
8. _____ good book (any good book) is always a pleasure for me.

ARTICLES

Indefinite and Definite

1. No article is used before the name of persons, countries, streets, cities, or towns when they are used as proper nouns.

> They live in Northbrook on Whitehall Court.
>
> Ms. Draper is going to Poland.

If such words are used as adjectives, they are preceded by an article.

> *Chicago* is a large city.
>
> *The Chicago fire* was very interesting.
>
> *Broadway* is very interesting.
>
> *The Broadway merchants* held a meeting.

Names of rivers, seas, mountain chains, and countries are preceded by *the* when they contain an adjective or some qualifying word.

> *the* Mississippi River   *the* Ural Mountains
>
> *the* Pacific Ocean   *the* United States

2. No article is used when a noun is modified by someone's name.

> Nancy's book   Pope John Paul's speech

No article is used when a noun is modified by a possessive pronoun.

> his hat   my book

3. Superlative adjectives (adjectives ending with -*est*) are preceded by *the*.

> Mount Everest is the *highest* mountain in the world.

Practice

A *Some of the blank spaces below require articles; others do not. Fill in the articles where needed.*

1. ___The___ air in this room is not fresh.

2. _____ fresh air is needed by all growing children.

3. _____ telephone rings very often in our office.

4. I always get on _____ bus at _____ same corner every morning.

5. Look! Lou is waving to us from across _____ street.

6. _____ some women from _____ Peru visited us.

7. _____ tea will not keep you awake at night.

8. However, _____ coffee seems to keep some people awake.

9. _____ tea in this pot is very weak.

10. _____ coffee which comes from Latin America is very good.

11. _____ cotton is one of _____ most important products of _____ South.

12. The U.S. Constitution guarantees _____ right to free speech.

13. Some of _____ important products which we import from _____ India are _____ tea, _____ cotton, and _____ rice.

14. _____ copper is _____ good conductor of _____ electricity.

15. Plenty of _____ rain and_____ sun are necessary for_____ raising of _____ cotton.

16. _____ sun is shining now, but part of _____ sky is still dark.

17. At times everyone must take _____ medicine.

18. _____ medicine which _____ doctor prescribed helped my cough.

19. He likes to study _____ history.

20. In that course, we study_____ history of all _____ western European countries.

21. _____ milk is my daughter's favorite drink.

22. I spilled _____ milk which was on the table.

ARTICLES

Indefinite and Definite

B *Some of the sentences require articles; others do not. Fill in the articles as required.*

1. We went to _____the_____ Statue of Liberty this summer.

2. When you go to _____ Chicago, be sure to visit _____ Sears Building.

3. She works in _____ building on _____ corner of Fifth Avenue and 72nd Street.

4. New York City is _____ largest city in _____ United States.

5. _____ traffic on _____ Madison Avenue is very heavy.

6. _____ Pittsburgh is _____ center of _____ steel industry of _____ Pennsylvania.

7. _____ Hudson River forms _____ boundary between _____ New York State and _____ New Jersey.

8. _____ Middle East is rich in _____ natural resources.

9. On our trip to _____ South America, we plan to stop off at _____ Haiti and _____ Dominican Republic.

10. _____ Great Wall of China is visible from outer space.

11. _____ rivers of _____ eastern part of _____ United States flow toward _____ Atlantic Ocean.

12. _____ machines which we ordered from _____ Pittsburgh arrived this morning.

13. The distance from _____ Washington, D.C., to _____ Minneapolis is about one thousand miles.

14. _____ largest river in _____ Germany is _____ Rhine.

15. _____ subways in Mexico City are very quiet.

16. _____ Bering Strait was once _____ land mass.

17. _____ climate of _____ southern Italy is very warm.

C *Fill in the articles where needed.*

1. _____The_____ chair on which you are sitting is uncomfortable.

2. _____ fire which destroyed _____ building started on _____ roof.

3. My family bought _____ new stove last week. It has _____ timer, _____ clock, and _____ light for _____ oven.

4. Please tell me about _____ book that you are reading.

Indefinite and Definite

5. I enjoyed _____ speech by _____ Mr. Chin last night. He spoke about _____ life in _____ China.

6. We all had _____ good time at _____ dance last night.

7. _____ price of _____ gold is rising, but _____ price of _____ silver is falling.

8. Much of _____ silver which we use in _____ United States comes from _____ Montana.

9. _____ drinking water often varies in taste, according to locality. _____ drinking water in New York City is very good.

10. They sell _____ interesting magazines at that store.

11. We often go to _____ zoo and watch _____ animals.

12. _____ candidates for mayor debated _____ crime problem.

13. Please open _____ windows. _____ air in this room is not good.

14. They plan to visit _____ Russia this summer. I understand _____ Russian language is difficult to learn.

15. Mr. and Mrs. Ames are now traveling in _____ South America. They plan to visit _____ Venezuela, _____ Colombia, _____ Peru, and _____ Argentina.

16. They will arrive in _____ Caracas around noon.

Future Tense

Another way (in addition to *will* + the simple form of the verb) to express the future is to use the appropriate form of *to be going to* and the simple form of the verb. The contracted forms are generally used.

I am (I'm) going to see	we are (we're) going to see
you are (you're) going to see	you are (you're) going to see
he is (he's) going to see	
she is (she's) going to see	they are (they're) going to see
it is (it's) going to see	

Practice

Complete the following sentences with the going to *form of the future using the verbs in parentheses. Use both the full form and the contracted form.*

1. They _are going to,___'re going to_ (visit) us next weekend.
2. We _____ (eat) out tonight.
3. I _____ (leave) for Nairobi on Tuesday.
4. They _____ (wait) for us after the show.
5. We _____ (get) up early tomorrow morning and go fishing.
6. She _____ (drive) to California.
7. We _____ (go) to Canada on our vacation.
8. You _____ (have) an exam in mathematics tomorrow.
9. They _____ (go) to Europe by plane.
10. Mike _____ (take) Alex to the dance tonight.
11. It _____ (be) difficult to reach him at this late hour.
12. I believe it _____ (rain).
13. Henry _____ (study) to be a doctor.
14. You _____ (stay) home tonight and watch television.
15. Mr. and Mrs. Blake _____ (build) a summer home on Merritt Island.
16. He _____ (start) his new job next week.
17. They _____ (move) the plant to the suburbs.

Past Tense

The past form of *going to* indicates an action which was planned or intended but which did not happen. Use the appropriate past tense form of *to be going to* and the simple form of the verb.

I was going to speak	we were going to speak
you were going to speak	you were going to speak
he was going to speak	
she was going to speak	they were going to speak
it was going to speak	

Practice

Substitute the past tense form of going to *for the verbs in italics.*

1. I *intended* to do it yesterday, but I was too busy. <u>*I was going to do it yesterday, but I was too busy.*</u>

2. We *intended* to go swimming, but the weather was too cold. _____

3. I *planned* to spend the evening on my homework but fell asleep right after dinner._____

4. They *intended* to spend the whole year abroad, but their money ran out._____

5. We *planned* to go by car but finally decided to go by plane. _____

6. You *planned* to give a big reception but then decided against it. _____

7. They *planned* to get married in June but then waited until October._____

8. At first he *intended* to ask Sally to the dance, but finally he invited Jane. _____

9. I *intended* to rewrite my exercises but didn't have enough time. _____

10. I *planned* to return your book today but left it at home. _____

11. They *planned* to leave for Europe last week, but Mrs. Ortiz was too ill to go. _____

12. At first she *intended* to put the boy in the elementary class, but later she put him in an advanced section. _____

13. We *planned* to go to a movie last night but were too tired._____

14. I *intended* to write to you several times, but something always interfered._____

PRESENT CONTINUOUS TENSE

Future Time

The present continuous tense, is often used to describe future plans which are definite. An adverb of time often accompanies such usage.

> She *is leaving* for Moscow next week.
>
> They *are returning* to their homelands when the semester ends.

Practice

Complete the following sentences by using the present continuous tense of the verbs in parentheses.

1. When _____*are*_____ you _____*leaving*_____ (leave) for Rome?
   I hear that Charlene _*is leaving*_ (leave) next Saturday.

2. My brother _____ (come) to visit me next week.

3. What time _____ you _____ (go) to the movies tonight? Ron says that he _____ (go) at nine o'clock.

4. Coretta _____ (fly) to England next Saturday.

5. When _____ Ms. Green _____ (come) to see you?

6. Tony says that he _____ (leave) for San Antonio on the fifteenth.

7. I _____ (go) to the seashore on my vacation.

8. Mr. Schwartz _____ (arrive) on Flight 109 this evening.

9. Where _____ you _____ (go) on your vacation? _____ your wife _____ (go) with you?

10. Mr. Zane _____ (leave) for Utah in the morning.

11. Some friends _____ (come) to visit us tonight.

12. She _____ (go) to Denver on Wednesday, but her husband _____ not _____ (go) until next week.

13. What bus _____ your friend _____ (arrive) on?

14. He _____ (come) in on a Trailways bus which arrives at eight o'clock.

15. Mr. Wyler _____ (fly) to Dallas on Saturday.

16. I _____ (leave) for Houston in the morning.

17. What train _____ Mr. North _____ (leave) on?

Negatives

Modal auxiliaries such as *can, may, must,* and *should* accompany main verbs. Form their negatives by placing *not* after the auxiliaries. The contracted forms *can't, mustn't,* and *shouldn't* are generally used, but note that no contraction is used with *may.*

She can speak English.	
She can*not* speak English.	She *can't* speak English.
We must go there.	
We must *not* go there.	We *mustn't* go there.
He may go to the movies.	
We should meet tomorrow.	We *shouldn't* meet tomorrow.
We should *not* meet tomorrow.	

Practice

Change the following sentences from affirmative to negative. Use both the full form and the contracted form (except for may).

1. We can meet you later. *We cannot meet you later. We can't meet you later.*

2. You may sit here. _____

3. We should tell her about it. _____

4. He may leave on Wednesday. _____

5. They can go by plane. _____

6. We must wait here. _____

7. I can understand him easily. _____

8. She should sit near the window. _____

9. We must do the same thing again. _____

10. She can play the piano well. _____

11. He can understand everything I say. _____

12. You should watch television every night. _____

13. She may pass her examination. _____

14. You can see him later. _____

15. You may fish here. _____

Yes-No Questions

Form *yes-no* questions with modal auxiliaries by placing the auxiliary before the subject.

She can speak English.	*Can she* speak English?
We should go there.	*Should we* go there?

Practice

Change the following statements to questions.

1. They should obey the rules. *Should they obey the rules?* _____

2. They both can speak English well. _____

3. Betsy should spend more time on her English. _____

4. We may sit in these chairs. _____

5. They can meet us at two o'clock. _____

6. I may call you later. _____

7. He should eat less meat. _____

8. He may tell her. _____

9. We should speak to her about it. _____

10. They may leave now. _____

11. You could go by plane. _____

12. You could send them a fax. _____

13. I should stay at home more. _____

14. Allan may wait in his office. _____

15. Al can go with us to the beach. _____

16. She could leave immediately. _____

Form information questions with modal auxiliaries by placing the auxiliary before the subject and adding a question word.

We should leave soon.	When should we leave?
He could be at the office.	Where could he be?

Practice

Change the following sentences to questions beginning with the question words in parentheses.

1. He can see her later. (When) *When can he see her?* _____

2. The babysitter could wait here. (Where) _____

3. You may study here. (Where) _____

4. You can eat here. (Where) _____

5. I can understand English very well. (How well) _____

6. You should be here at three o'clock. (What time) _____

7. We should tell her about the sale. (What) _____

8. He can meet us in the store. (Where) _____

9. The children must come home early. (When) _____

10. They can hang their coats in the closet. (Where) _____

11. I should tell her the truth. (What) _____

12. You must be here at one o'clock. (What time) _____

13. Karen should sit near the blackboard. (Where) _____

14. We should finish this before 3:00. (What time) _____

15. Gabriel can speak five languages. (How many) _____

16. You must do this first. (What) _____

SHORT ANSWERS

Short answers are the most common way of answering *yes-no* questions. A short answer consists of the subject of the sentence and an auxiliary verb or part of *to be*.

Can you play the piano?	Yes, I can.	No, I can't.
Does she know the answer?	Yes, she does.	No, she doesn't.
Are they coming?	Yes, they are.	No, they aren't.

Pronouns generally replace nouns in short answers.

Will Ms. Wong be here soon?	Yes, she will.	No, she won't.
Did it rain yesterday?	Yes, it did.	No, it didn't.

Practice

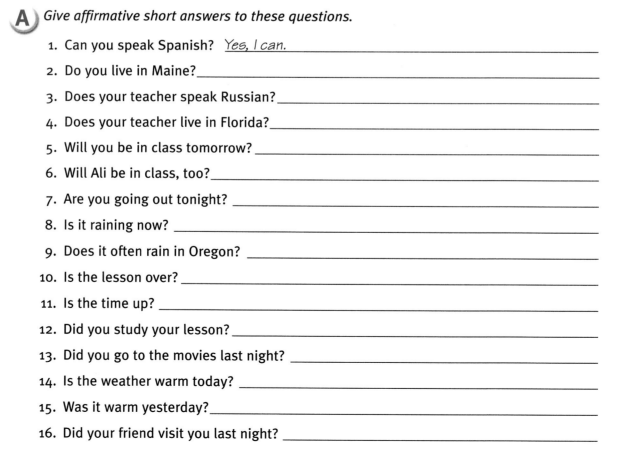

A *Give affirmative short answers to these questions.*

1. Can you speak Spanish? _Yes, I can._____

2. Do you live in Maine?_____

3. Does your teacher speak Russian?_____

4. Does your teacher live in Florida?_____

5. Will you be in class tomorrow? _____

6. Will Ali be in class, too?_____

7. Are you going out tonight? _____

8. Is it raining now? _____

9. Does it often rain in Oregon? _____

10. Is the lesson over? _____

11. Is the time up? _____

12. Did you study your lesson?_____

13. Did you go to the movies last night? _____

14. Is the weather warm today? _____

15. Was it warm yesterday?_____

16. Did your friend visit you last night? _____

17. Is today Friday? _____

18. Was yesterday Thursday? _____

19. Will tomorrow be Sunday? _____

20. May I open the window? _____

21. Can you fly an airplane? _____

22. Did it rain yesterday?_____

23. Did you study yesterday? _____

24. Were you busy yesterday?_____

25. Will you be busy tomorrow? _____

26. Is Washington a beautiful city?_____

B *Give negative short answers to the questions in Exercise A.*

Can you speak Spanish? *No, I can't.* _____

ADJECTIVES AND ADVERBS

Descriptive adjectives modify nouns.

> *a large* tree   an *open* door

Adverbs of manner modify verbs. They tell *how* we do something.

> **He speaks *slowly*.   They work *rapidly*.**

We can form many adverbs by adding *ly* to an adjective.

soft	softly
careful	carefully
easy (y to i)	easily

We can use a few words like *fast, hard, late,* and *low* as either adjectives or adverbs without any changes in form.

> **He is a *hard* worker.   He works *hard*.**

Practice

Supply the appropriate form of the adjective or adverb.

1. She is a ____*careful*____ (careful) student. She always does her homework ____*carefully*____ (careful).

2. The baseball player hit the ball _____ (hard).

3. Come _____ (quick). We need your help.

4. You should drive _____ (slow) along this dangerous road.

5. The old man walks very _____ (slow).

6. Pam is a very _____ (slow) learner.

7. Her brother, on the other hand, learns _____ (rapid).

8. Mr. Gonzalez has a _____ (permanent) visa.

9. He hopes to remain in this country _____ (permanent).

10. This is an _____ (easy) exercise.

11. I can do all of these exercises _____ (easy).

12. Ada works very _____ (hard) in her new job.

13. You walk very _____ (fast).

14. We are both _____ (serious) employees.

15. We both study English very _____ (serious).

16. I agree with you _____ (complete) in that matter.

17. This apple is very _____ (soft).

18. She always speaks _____ (soft) to the child.

19. Pete is a _____ (beautiful) kitten.

20. My sister plays the violin _____ (beautiful).

ADJECTIVES AND ADVERBS

Good, Well

Good is an adjective and must modify a noun.

> **She is a *good* student.**

Well is usually used as an adverb.

> **She works *well*.**

Well is occasionally used as an adjective. It is used as an adjective only when it means *to be in good health*.

> **John was sick, but now he is *well*.**

Practice

Supply good *or* well *in the following sentences.*

1. He does his work ___well___.

2. He plays the piano very _____.

3. He is a _____ pianist.

4. This pen does not work _____.

5. Our lunch today was very _____.

6. These exercises are _____ for us.

7. I was sick for a few days, but now I am _____ again.

8. How do you feel? _____ , thank you.

9. This new pen writes _____.

10. It is really a very _____ pen.

11. When you don't feel _____ , take a long walk. It is often a _____ medicine.

12. We congratulated him on his _____ work.

13. Ray plays tennis _____.

14. His brother is also a _____ tennis player.

15. The movie last night was really _____.

16. She speaks French _____.

Good, Well

17. She is a _____ student of mathematics.

18. Everything that she does, she does _____.

19. Dave dances _____.

20. His sister is also a _____ dancer.

21. I don't understand him _____ when he speaks so rapidly.

22. The weather today is very _____.

Comparative Form

The comparative form of one-syllable adjectives and adverbs adds *er*.

cold ⟶ cold*er*	soon ⟶ soon*er*
smart ⟶ smart*er*	fast ⟶ fast*er*

The comparative form of two-syllable adjectives and adverbs ending in *y* usually adds *er* (the *y* changes to *i*).

happy ⟶ happi*er*
easy ⟶ easi*er*

The comparative form of adjectives and adverbs of two or more syllables usually uses *more*.

difficult ⟶ *more difficult*	quickly ⟶ *more quickly*
beautiful ⟶ *more beautiful*	carefully ⟶ *more carefully*

Some adjectives and adverbs are irregular.

good ⟶ *better*	well ⟶ *better*
bad ⟶ *worse*	badly ⟶ *worse*

The comparative form of adjectives and adverbs is followed by *than*.

> She is *taller than* her sister.
>
> He drives *more carefully than* his brother [does].

Practice

A *Complete these sentences by supplying the comparative form of the adjective or adverb in parentheses. Be sure to include the word* than.

1. He is _younger_ (young) _than_ I [am].

2. Carmen is much _____ (old) _____ expected.

3. Alaska is _____ (big) _____ Delaware.

4. This book is _____ (good) _____ the last one we used.

Comparative Form

5. The weather this winter is _____ (bad) _____ the weather last winter.

6. This exercise is _____ (difficult) _____ the last one.

7. This metal is _____ (valuable) _____ gold.

8. Jane is _____ (attractive) _____ her sister.

9. He goes there _____ (often) _____ I.

10. They go to the movies _____ (frequently) _____ you.

11. I get up every morning much _____ (late) _____ you.

B *Complete these sentences by supplying the comparative form of the adjective or adverb in parentheses. Be sure to include the word* than.

1. She speaks _____more_____ (rapidly) _____than_____ I.

2. He prepares his homework _____ (carefully) _____ most students.

3. She works _____ (hard) _____ her sister.

4. We stayed _____ (long) _____ we expected.

5. Our troops fought _____ (bravely) _____ anyone expected.

6. The time passed _____ (quickly) _____ I expected.

7. The speaker spoke _____ (loud) _____ was really necessary.

8. They arrived _____ (soon) _____ we.

9. The weather today is _____ (warm) _____ the weather yesterday.

10. John's car was much _____ (expensive) _____ my car.

11. This contract is _____ (satisfactory) _____ the previous one.

12. This street is even _____ (wide) _____ the highway.

13. These exercises are _____ (complicated) _____ some of the others.

14. The climate of Caracas is _____ (good) _____ that of Maracaibo.

15. Lil is much _____ (clever) _____ her brother.

16. This summer is _____ (hot) _____ last summer.

17. She spoke _____ (fluently) _____ expected.

ADJECTIVES AND ADVERBS

Superlative Form

The superlative form of one-syllable adjectives and adverbs adds *est*.

cold ⟶ cold*est*   soon ⟶ soon*est*

smart ⟶ smart*est*   fast ⟶ fast*est*

The superlative form of two-syllable adjectives and adverbs ending in *y* usually adds *est* (the *y* changes to *i*).

pretty ⟶ the pretti*est*

funny ⟶ the funni*est*

The superlative form of adjectives and adverbs of two or more syllables usually uses *most*.

difficult ⟶ most difficult   quickly ⟶ most quickly

beautiful ⟶ most beautiful   carefully ⟶ most carefully

The superlative form of some adjectives and adverbs is irregular.

good ⟶ best   well ⟶ best

bad ⟶ worst   badly ⟶ worst

The superlative form of all adjectives and adverbs is preceded by *the*.

She is *the tallest* girl in the class.

He drives *the most carefully* of anyone in the family.

Practice

Supply the superlative form of the adjective or adverb in parentheses. Be sure to use the word the.

1. She speaks *the most rapidly* (rapidly) of any of my friends.

2. This is _____ (expensive) book that I own.

3. George is _____ (bad) student in the class.

4. The *Herald* is _____ (important) newspaper in the town.

5. Robin works _____ (hard) of all the ballerinas in the troupe.

6. He is _____ (ambitious) man that I know.

7. Of the three brothers, Malcolm wakes up _____ (late).

8. Rebecca swims _____ (gracefully) of all the team members.

9. She is _____ (intelligent) person that I know.

10. The story which you told was _____ (sad) of all.

11. January is _____ (cold) month of the year.

12. Which is _____ (good) route from Miami to New York?

PAST CONTINUOUS TENSE

Form the past continuous tense with the past tense of *to be* and the present participle (*ing* form) of the main verb.

I was working	we were working
you were working	you were working
he was working	
she was working	they were working
it was working	

The past continuous tense describes a past action which was going on when another action took place.

I *was sleeping* when you called.

They *were eating* dinner when we arrived.

Practice

A *Supply the correct past continuous tense form of the verbs in parentheses.*

1. They _were eating_ (eat) in the restaurant on the corner when I saw them.

2. It _____ (rain) when I left home.

3. When you telephoned, I _____ (have) dinner.

4. They _____ (travel) in Australia when they heard the news.

5. The baby _____ (sleep) soundly when I went to wake him.

6. He _____ just _____ (order) breakfast when I went to his hotel room.

7. I got sick while we _____ (drive) to my grandmother's.

8. He _____ (work) in California when his father died.

9. I _____ (take) a nap when you called.

10. She _____ (talk) with Mr. Samuels when I saw her in the hall.

11. The accident happened while they _____ (travel) in Greece.

12. The flight attendant fell as he _____ (get) into a taxi.

13. The car _____ (travel) at high speed when it approached the corner.

B *In the following sentences, supply the past tense or the past continuous tense form of the verbs in parentheses as required by the meaning.*

1. I _studied_ (study) very diligently last night.

2. I _was studying_ (study) last night when you called me on the phone.

3. While I _____ (go) home last night, I saw a bad accident.

4. I _____ (go) home last night by bus.

5. We _____ (drive) to an amusement park yesterday.

6. We _____ (drive) at about forty miles an hour when the accident happened.

7. We _____ (have) our dinner when you phoned.

8. We _____ (have) our dinner in a restaurant last night.

9. While I _____ (come) to work this morning, I met an old friend.

10. I _____ (come) to work in a taxi this morning.

11. The wind _____ (blow) hard when I came to work this morning.

12. The wind _____ (blow) hard this morning.

13. It _____ (rain) hard last night.

14. It _____ (rain) hard when I left the office at five o'clock.

15. The sun _____ (shine) brightly when I got up this morning.

16. The sun _____ (shine) brightly this morning.

17. At seven o'clock, when you telephoned, I _____ (read) the newspaper.

18. I _____ (read) two books last week.

19. I _____ (sleep) soundly when the phone rang.

20. I _____ (sleep) soundly last night.

21. June _____ (play) the piano when I arrived.

C *Supply either the past tense or the past continuous tense form of the verbs in parentheses as required by the meaning.*

1. As I _was walking_ (walk) home yesterday, I ___met___ (meet) a woman who ___asked___ (ask) me for directions to the subway.

2. It _____ (rain) hard when I _____ (leave) home this morning.

3. Pete _____ (fall) and _____ (hurt) himself when he _____ (ride) his bicycle yesterday.

4. At five o'clock, when I _____ (call) the Kennedy's home, they _____ (have) dinner.

5. Sophia _____ (drive) to work when she _____ (hear) the news on the radio.

6. We _____ (sit) on our front porch when Ms. Gold _____ (drive) up in her new car.

7. As Terri _____ (get) out of the taxi, she _____ (slip) and _____ (break) her leg.

8. Mr. Cash _____ (drive) at about forty miles an hour when the accident _____ (happen).

9. Your message _____ (come) just as I _____ (leave) my home.

10. Last night, just as we _____ (leave) for the movies, some friends _____ (drop) by.

11. Nelson _____ (talk) with his boss when I last _____ (see) him.

12. At noon, when you _____ (telephone), I _____ (work) in my garden.

D *Change each of the following sentences from the past tense to the past continuous tense. Add any words, phrases, or clauses which you may need in order to complete the meaning of the sentence.*

1. I studied my English lesson last night. *I was studying my English lesson last night when my friend called me.*

2. I talked to Maurice Cooper this morning._____

3. Tony walked home from work yesterday afternoon. _____

4. She ate her dinner._____

5. I finished my work._____

6. Larry spoke to Ms. Watkins about a raise. _____

7. I wrote a letter last night. _____

8. He lived in Africa. _____

9. They got off the bus at Broad Street._____

10. We had lunch with Mr. and Mrs. Chambers. _____

11. Chris left home this morning. _____

12. Dr. Berger had a haircut. _____

13. Sharon typed her term paper. _____

14. I visited the Andersons._____

15. The puppy cried. _____

Form the future continuous tense by using *will be* and the present participle (*ing* form) of the main verb. The contracted forms are generally used.

> Singular:
>
> I will be working ⟶ I'll be working
>
> You will be working ⟶ You'll be working
>
> He will be working ⟶ He'll be working
>
> She will be working ⟶ She'll be working
>
> It will be working ⟶ It'll be working

> Plural:
>
> We will be working ⟶ We'll be working
>
> You will be working ⟶ You'll be working
>
> They will be working ⟶ They'll be working

The future continuous tense describes an action that will be going on when another action takes place.

> I *will be studying* when you return this evening.
>
> They' *ll be traveling* in Germany by the time you arrive here.

Practice

Supply the future continuous tense of the verbs in parentheses.

1. If you come at noon, we <u>will be eating</u> (eat) lunch.

2. At this time next month, we _____ (travel) in South America.

3. At ten o'clock tomorrow morning, I _____ (have) my music lesson.

4. I _____ (wait) on the corner for you at the usual time.

5. If you call her at six, she probably _____ (practice) the piano.

6. It probably _____ (rain) when you get back.

7. If you come before six, I _____ (work) in my garden.

8. Tomorrow afternoon at this time, we _____ (fly) over the Caribbean.

9. Don't call him after seven. He _____ (watch) his favorite television program.

10. Don't call her after lunch. She _____ (take) her usual afternoon nap.

11. At this time next year, he _____ (study) at the University of Illinois.

Much is used with noncountable nouns; that is, things that cannot be counted and do not have a plural form.

These nouns do not normally have plural forms.

much sugar	*much* rain	*much* coffee

Much is usually used in negative sentences and questions.

> I don't have *much* money.
>
> Do you need *much* time?

Many is used with plural countable nouns.

> *many* cups of sugar
>
> *many* students

A lot of is used interchangeably with *much* and *many*. *A lot of* is the most commonly used term of these three.

a lot of sugar	*a lot of* books	*a lot of* love

In questions with How, *much* and *many* are used. *A lot of* is not used.

> How *much* milk did you buy?
>
> How *many* chairs will we need?

Practice

 A *Complete the following sentences with* much *or* many.

1. There aren't ___*many*___ large factories in this town.

2. He doesn't spend _____ time on his English.

3. Does this factory produce _____ different kinds of products?

4. Does she spend _____ money on clothes?

5. Is there _____ oil in Venezuela?

6. He doesn't drink _____ milk.

7. Does he have _____ friends in this office?

8. There aren't _____ mountains in that part of the country.

9. There isn't _____ milk in this pitcher.

10. How _____ time do you spend on your English every day?

11. How _____ windows are there in your office?

12. How _____ times a week do you go to the movies?

13. How _____ money do you spend on magazines each month?

14. He doesn't make _____ mistakes in spelling.

B *In which of the sentences in Exercise A can you substitute* a lot of *for* much *or* many?

ALSO, TOO, EITHER

Also and *too* change to *either* in negative sentences.

> I want to come too.
>
> I don't want to come *either.*

> They also want this book.
>
> They don't want this book *either.*

Practice

 A *Change the following sentences from affirmative to negative.*

1. Mary likes to study with our group, too. *Mary doesn't like to study with our group either.*
   _____

2. John also likes to play tennis. _____

3. They also want to move to the suburbs. _____

4. Richard will also come. _____

5. He eats in that restaurant too. _____

6. We can also play baseball. _____

7. He also likes American food. _____

8. She is able to hear him too. _____

9. My parents like to listen to the radio too. _____

10. Mr. Johnson is also a tennis player. _____

11. Molly can also play this game. _____

12. This book was also expensive. _____

B *Change the following sentences from negative to affirmative.*

1. Mike doesn't know her well either. *He also knows her well. He knows her well too.*

2. She doesn't like to watch television either. _____

3. Helen cannot swim well either. _____

4. The manager wasn't able to speak to him either. _____

5. They don't want to live in the suburbs either. _____

6. My sister won't be back before noon either. _____

7. He doesn't come to work by bus either. _____

8. Rachel isn't a friendly person either. _____

Use *any* in negative sentences; use *some* in affirmative sentences.

> Gerald took *some* books home with him.
>
> Gerald didn't take *any* books home with him.

Practice

A *Change the following sentences from affirmative to negative.*

1. There are some extra chairs in the next room. *There aren't any extra chairs in the next room.*

2. We saw some good shows in New York. _____

3. He made some mistakes in addition. _____

4. They have some pretty dresses in that store. _____

5. The teacher taught us some important grammar rules. _____

6. We learned some new words in class yesterday. _____

7. There are some flowers in the yellow vase. _____

8. There are some rich men in this town. _____

9. We have some good neighbors. _____

B *Change the following sentences from negative to affirmative.*

1. I didn't see any good shows on TV last night. *I saw some good shows on TV last night.*

2. Don't pour me any coffee. _____

3. We don't need any more chairs in this room. _____

4. There aren't any tables in the hall. _____

5. She doesn't want any oranges. _____

6. They didn't tell us about any of their experiences. _____

7. There aren't any good seats left for the play tonight. _____

8. You won't need any winter clothes in San Diego. _____

9. I don't have any more money. _____

C Complete the following sentences with some or any.

1. I don't have ___any___ money with me.

2. Please give me _____ more coffee.

3. I'm sorry, but there isn't _____ more coffee.

4. The baby is asleep. Please don't make _____ noise.

5. We need _____ oranges for breakfast.

6. I'm sorry, but I didn't have _____ time to prepare my lessons last night.

7. There aren't _____ seats available in the waiting room.

8. He never makes _____ mistakes in spelling.

9. I wanted to buy _____ fresh eggs, but there weren't _____ in the store.

10. I didn't have _____ stamps, so I went to the post office to buy _____.

11. They are having _____ trouble with their new car.

12. I never have _____ trouble with my car.

13. The teacher won't find _____ mistakes in Pat's addition.

14. She will surely find _____ in my addition.

15. I tried to borrow _____ money from him, but he said he didn't have _____.

16. She never gives the poor dog _____ water to drink.

17. Don't give _____ money to Ron. He doesn't deserve _____.

18. There aren't _____ patients in the waiting room at the moment.

19. Please put _____ water in that vase; the flowers are dying.

20. I wanted some fruit, but nobody had _____.

21. Sandy says she never has _____ fruit.

22. There are _____ famous museums in Mexico City, but we didn't have time to visit _____.

23. He never gives his patients _____ candy.

24. The doctor gave me _____ medicine for my cough.

ANYONE, SOMEONE

Use *anybody, anyone, anything,* and *anywhere* in negative sentences.
Use *somebody, someone, something,* and *somewhere* in affirmative sentences.

> **We heard *someone* enter the darkened room.**
>
> **We didn't hear *anything* in the dark.**

Practice

A *Change the following sentences from affirmative to negative.*

1. He told us something about his trip. *He didn't tell us anything about his trip.*

2. There is someone at the door. _____

3. You left something on the hall table. _____

4. Bob will bring someone with him. _____

5. I lost the book somewhere downtown. _____

6. There is somebody in the next room. _____

7. Bobbie went somewhere last night with her boss. _____

8. He has something important to say to you. _____

B *Change the following sentences from negative to affirmative.*

1. He doesn't know anything about the plan. *He knows something about the plan.*

2. There isn't anything wrong with Toby's ear. _____

3. There wasn't anyone at the door. _____

4. We haven't spoken to anybody about it. _____

5. There doesn't seem to be anybody in the office. _____

6. My keys aren't anywhere in this room. _____

7. I don't think there is anything wrong with the printer. _____

8. They didn't find her anywhere. _____

I—my—mine	we—our—ours
you—your—yours	you—your—yours
he—his—his	
she—her—hers	they—their—theirs
it—its—its	

This is *my* ring.	That is *our* truck.
This ring is *mine*.	This truck is *ours*.

Practice

 A *Substitute the appropriate possessive pronouns for the word in italics.*

1. This pen is *my pen*. *This pen is mine.* _____

2. These seats are *our seats*._____

3. This umbrella is *her umbrella*. _____

4. These pencils are *your pencils*._____

5. That computer is *my father's computer.* _____

6. That overcoat is *his overcoat.* _____

7. These magazines seem to be *your magazines;* they are not *my magazines.* _____

8. I believe this pen is *her pen;* it is not *my pen*._____

9. Is this notebook *your notebook* or Sarah's? _____

10. Is this dictionary *your dictionary* or William's? _____

11. This pair of scissors is *her pair of scissors.* _____

12. These seats are *their seats;* they are not *our seats.* _____

13. This book is *your book;* the one over there on the desk is *my book.* _____

14. He drives his car to work every day and I drive *my car.* _____

15. You take care of your things, and I'll take care of *my things*._____

16. Their home is pretty, but *our home* is prettier. _____

17. His pronunciation is bad, and *my pronunciation* is too. _____

18. His car was expensive, but *your car* was more expensive. _____

B *In the following sentences substitute the verb* to be *for the verb* to belong. *Then introduce a possessive pronoun or the possessive form of the noun.*

1. This book *belongs* to him. *This book is his.* _____

2. This pencil *belongs* to Anthony. *This pencil is Anthony's.* _____

3. That notebook *belongs* to her. _____

4. That umbrella *belongs* to me. _____

5. I'm sure this pen *belongs* to Adrian. _____

6. No, it *belongs* to Miss Jefferson. _____

7. These magazines *belong* to them. _____

8. These pencils *belong* to us. _____

9. These books *belong* to them. _____

10. This book doesn't *belong* to me. _____

11. This pen *belongs* to him. _____

12. I think this desk *belongs* to Mrs. Jones. _____

13. That car *belongs* to Robert. _____

14. These green apples *belong* to us, but those yellow ones *belong* to them. _____

15. I think this pencil *belongs* to me, but the yellow one *belongs* to you. _____

16. This box of candy must *belong* to him. _____

17. This umbrella *belongs* to the teacher. _____

18. These seats *belong* to them. _____

19. That black sports car *belongs* to our landlord. _____

20. This watch doesn't *belong* to me; it *belongs* to my father. _____

21. The red sweater *belongs* to me; the blue one *belongs* to Virginia. _____

22. That bicycle *belongs* to Jim's little brother. _____

C *Complete the following sentences with either a possessive adjective or a possessive pronoun.*

1. Jeremy lost ____*his*____ pen. Will you please lend him __*yours*__ ?
2. I was on time for _____ class, but Helen was late for _____.
3. They have _____ methods of travel and we have _____.
4. We naturally prefer _____ methods, and they naturally prefer _____.
5. I found _____ notebook, but Jack couldn't find _____.
6. They think that _____ home is the prettiest on the block, and we think _____ is.
7. I left _____ pen at home. May I borrow _____ for a moment?
8. He drives to work in _____ car, and she drives to work in _____.
9. Tell William not to forget to bring _____ tennis racket, and don't forget to bring _____.
10. They swim in _____ pool and we swim in _____.
11. I have _____ vacation in June and Fern has _____ in July.
12. I found _____ umbrella, but Jill couldn't find _____.
13. We were late for _____ class, and Hope and Gwen were also late for _____.
14. Ted enjoys _____ work and I enjoy _____.
15. Each student in the school has _____ own desk and _____ own locker.
16. I borrowed money from all _____ friends, but Peg refused to borrow any money from _____.
17. We have a television set in _____ bedroom, and the boys have another set in _____.
18. Where are you going on _____ vacation? I hope to spend _____ in Europe.
19. They have _____ ideas on such matters, and we have _____.
20. We spend _____ money in one way; they spend _____ in another way.

REFLEXIVE PRONOUNS

myself	ourselves
yourself	yourselves
himself	
herself	} themselves
itself	

Reflexive pronouns refer back to the subject of the sentence. The subject and object are the same person (people).

> The man wounded *himself*.   The woman burned *herself*.

Practice

Supply the necessary reflexive pronouns.

1. The little girl hurt _____*herself*_____ when she fell.

2. We protect _____ from the rain with an umbrella.

3. My son taught _____ to sew.

4. Both boys taught _____ to swim.

5. We all enjoyed _____ at the concert last night.

6. The children are amusing _____ with the kitten.

7. The policewoman shot _____ by accident.

8. Did you enjoy _____ at the party last night?

9. You will cut _____ with that knife if you are not careful.

10. I once cut _____ badly with the same knife.

11. I blame _____ for all that trouble.

12. She likes to look at _____ in the mirror.

13. My father cuts _____ every morning when he shaves.

14. Joy cut _____ on a piece of glass.

15. My daughter is not old enough to dress _____.

16. The dog hurt _____ when it jumped over the fence.

Reflexive pronouns are also used to give emphasis to some person or thing mentioned in the sentence.

> I *myself* will do the work.
>
> The car *itself* was undamaged.
>
> They are going to have to fix the motor *themselves*.

Practice

Supply the necessary reflexive pronouns.

1. Claude _____ *himself* _____ will make all the preparations for the trip.

2. I _____ will have little to do.

3. Amy said that she _____ saw the man enter the office.

4. The policeman _____ shot the thief.

5. We _____ made the first offer to buy the business.

6. The president _____ will deliver the principal address.

7. She says that she _____ will be responsible for the debt.

8. I _____ refused to take part in the matter.

9. The boys _____ will cut the grass once a week.

10. The captain _____ led the attack against the enemy.

11. The pupils _____ decorated the classroom with flags and flowers.

12. The detective _____ committed the murder.

13. I _____ don't like that restaurant.

14. It was you _____ who recommended it so highly.

15. They _____ will provide the money.

16. Jack _____ mailed the letter.

17. They _____ arranged the matter in that form.

18. You _____ must speak to him about it.

19. Janet said that she would arrange for the flowers _____.

20. I don't want to do it, but I guess I'll have to go _____.

Reflexive pronouns used with *by* mean *alone* or *without help*.

She lives by *herself*.	(She lives with no other people.)
He built this house by *himself*.	(No one helped him.)

Practice

In place of the word alone, *substitute the preposition* by *and the required reflexive pronoun.*

1. He went for a walk in the park alone. *He went for a walk in the park by himself.*

2. They made the long trip through the woods alone. _____

3. I don't like to go to the movies alone. _____

4. Kim, however, prefers to go to the movies alone. _____

5. Joe likes to take long walks in the woods alone. _____

6. The old man lives alone in a cabin in the woods. _____

7. Hal works alone in a small office. _____

8. My aunt, although she is elderly, prefers to live alone. _____

9. Do you like to eat alone? _____

10. I went to the opera last night alone. _____

11. The girls study alone in one group and the boys study alone in a second group. _____

12. One shouldn't spend too much time alone. _____

13. She sits alone and stares out the window all day long. _____

14. I can finish this work alone. _____

15. He prefers to do his homework alone. _____

16. The dog found its way home alone. _____

17. He plans to make a trip to Canada alone. _____

18. The wagon seemed to roll down the street alone. _____

19. We always enjoyed steering the boat alone. _____

20. You should try to answer the questions alone. _____

Form the present perfect tense with *have (has)* and the past participle of the main verb. The past participle of all regular verbs is the same as the past tense form: walked, talked, studied, etc. The past participles of irregular verbs are often very irregular and must simply be memorized. (See Quick Grammar Reference for complete list.)

I have worked	we have worked
you have worked	you have worked
he/she/it/has worked	they have worked

The present perfect tense often describes an action that happened at an indefinite time in the past.

I *have read* that book.	They *have moved* to Los Angeles.

The present perfect tense also describes an action that was repeated several times in the past.

I *have read* that book several times.	He *has studied* this lesson over and over.

Practice

Supply the present perfect tense form of the verbs in parentheses.

1. I _have spoken_ (speak) to him about it several times.

2. We _____ (finish) all our homework.

3. He _____ (visit) us many times.

4. She _____ (return) my book at last.

5. I am afraid that I _____ (lose) my car keys.

6. We _____ (be) in Florida many times.

7. It _____ (rain) a lot this year.

8. We _____ (learn) many new words in this course.

9. We _____ (tell) Ed what you said.

10. They _____ (hear) that story before.

11. We _____ (lend) money to them several times.

12. Mr. Katz _____ (go) to Tokyo to work.

The simple past tense is most often used when a sentence mentions or implies the exact time of an action. When the present perfect tense is used to describe an action which happened at an indefinite time in the past, the sentence does not usually mention the exact time of the action.

Past:	He *went* to Boston yesterday.
Present Perfect:	He *has gone* to Boston several times.

Past:	I *was* here last night.
Present Perfect:	I *have been* here before.

Past:	I *visited* that museum when I was downtown last week.
Present Perfect:	I *have visited* that museum.

Practice

Supply either the simple past tense or the present perfect tense form as required by the meaning.

1. I _____went_____ (go) to bed late last night; I ___have done___ (do) this many times lately.

2. Mr. Ashe _____ (go) to Chicago last week.

3. I _____(read) that book several times.

4. I first _____ (read) it while I was on my vacation last summer.

5. I _____ (be) in Norfolk many times.

6. Mr. Dale _____ (have) little experience in teaching that subject.

7. Billy _____ (fall) as he was crossing the street.

8. I _____ (see) Diane a few days ago.

9. When the bell rang, Wade _____ (jump) from his seat and _____ (run) from the room.

10. I _____ (try) that restaurant again and again, but I do not like the food there.

11. When I was young, I often _____ (go) fishing with my father.

12. I _____ (complete) my paper at last.

The present perfect tense also describes actions that began in the past and have continued up to the present.

> **He has worked here for two years. (He is still working here.)**
>
> **They have lived here since June. (They are still living here.)**

Note the difference in meaning between the following sentences:

> **He has worked here for two years. (He is still working here.)**
>
> **He worked here for two years. (He doesn't work here anymore.)**

Practice

Supply either the simple past tense or the present perfect tense form as required by the meaning.

1. I ____*moved*____ (move) to Pine Street in March; I ____*have lived*____ (live) there for three months now.

2. We _____ (live) in Washington from 1995 to 2000.

3. Before he came to the United States, Emil _____ (work) as a carpenter.

4. Since coming here, however, he _____ (work) as a clerk.

5. My former teacher was Miss Coe. I _____ (study) with her for one year.

6. My present teacher is Mr. Ming. I _____ (study) with him for six months.

7. Juanita Chávez speaks English well because she _____ (speak) English all her life.

8. Earl _____ (work) hard all his life. (He is dead.)

9. Eric _____ (work) hard all his life. (He is alive.)

10. Ms. Pate _____ (leave) New York last month and _____ (work) in Pittsburgh since then.

11. Gail, who is now in college, _____ (study) English for ten years.

12. I myself _____ (study) English steadily since 1998.

13. Henry, who is now in the hospital, _____ (be) there for several weeks.

14. When I saw her, Linda _____ (feel) ill.

Form the present perfect continuous tense with *have (has) been* and the present participle of the main verb.

I have been working	we have been working
you have been working	you have been working
he has been working	
she has been working	they have been working
it has been working	

The present perfect continuous tense describes an action that began in the past and has continued up to the present. In many cases it can be used interchangeably with the present perfect tense.

> They *have lived* here for five years.
>
> They *have been living* here for five years.

Practice

Change these present perfect tense verbs from the simple to the continuous form.

1. He has worked in that firm for many years. *He has been working in that firm for many years.*
2. They have talked for more than an hour. _____
3. I have traveled all over Europe. _____
4. He has slept for more than ten hours. _____
5. It has rained all day long. _____
6. He has studied English for many years. _____
7. We have used this textbook since January. _____
8. She has taught science for ten years. _____
9. They have lived in Dallas since 2001. _____
10. The two nations have quarreled for many years. _____
11. She has taken good care of her pets. _____
12. They have looked everywhere for the thief. _____
13. He has done very little work recently. _____
14. Lynn has worked very hard recently. _____
15. You have argued about that for more than an hour. _____

Negatives and Questions

Form negatives with the present perfect and present perfect continuous tenses by placing *not* after *have (has)*. The contractions *haven't* and *hasn't* are generally used.

They have *not* lived there long.	They *haven't* lived there long.
It has *not* been raining.	It *hasn't* been raining.

Form *yes-no* questions with these perfect tenses by placing *have (has)* before the subject.

Have they lived there long?	*Has* it been raining?

Practice

 A *Change the following sentences from affirmative to negative. Use both the full form and the contracted form.*

1. You have worked very hard at your job. *You have not worked very hard at your job.*
   You haven't worked very hard at your job.

2. She has been teaching there many years. _____

3. It has been snowing. _____

4. I have spoken to Ms. Wolf about it. _____

5. You have been studying computer science. _____

6. He has been the best student in the class. _____

7. She has been taking music lessons. _____

8. They have been discussing the matter all day long. _____

9. She has been sick since Wednesday. _____

10. They have returned home. _____

11. He has known her a long time. _____

12. Joel has found his pen. _____

13. You have been absent from class all week. _____

14. He has told her all about it. _____

15. Garvin has left for San Francisco. _____

16. They have been having trouble with their new car. _____

Negatives and Questions

17. He has been feeling well recently. _____

18. They have been married a long time. _____

B *Change the sentences in Exercise A to questions.*

You have worked very hard at your job. *Have you worked very hard at your job?*

Form information questions with the present perfect and present perfect continuous tenses by placing *have (has)* before the subject and adding a question word.

> *How long has* Gabriel worked here?
>
> *How long have* we been waiting?

Practice

Change the following sentences to questions beginning with How long.

1. He has been working for that firm for ten years. *How long has he been working for that firm?*

2. They have been married for five years. _____

3. They have been living in that same house for twenty years. _____

4. He has been absent from work for two weeks. _____

5. She has been studying computer science since June. _____

6. They have been arguing for more than an hour. _____

7. They have been friends for years. _____

8. He has been teaching computer science ever since he graduated from college. _____

9. It has been raining like this for an hour. _____

10. She has been a citizen since January. _____

11. He has been attending that college for four years. _____

12. They have occupied that same apartment for ten years. _____

13. He has been doing that same kind of work for many years. _____

14. She has been in the hospital for two months. _____

15. They have been driving that same car ever since I have known them. _____

16. The dog has been lying in that corner since this morning. _____

17. He has been manager of the department since February. _____

18. She has been waiting for him for an hour. _____

For shows the length of time of the action.

> **He has worked there *for* six months.**

Since shows the time that the action began.

> **He has worked there *since* February.**

Practice

A *Change these sentences to introduce* since *in place of* for. *Then make whatever other changes are necessary.*

1. She has been sick for three days. _She has been sick since Wednesday._

2. We have been living here for three years. _____

3. Sue has worked for that firm for six months. _____

4. I have not seen him for several days. _____

5. I have not eaten anything for two days. _____

6. We have been planning this trip for a year. _____

7. It has been raining steadily for eight hours. _____

8. I have not smoked a cigarette for two years. _____

9. We have been waiting for you for two hours. _____

10. He has been in the hospital for almost a month. _____

B *Change these sentences to introduce* for *instead of* since. *Then make whatever other changes are necessary.*

1. He has been absent since Monday. _He has been absent for three days._

2. We haven't seen them since February. _____

3. We have lived in the same house since 2002. _____

4. They have been friends since high school. _____

5. It has been snowing steadily since last night. _____

6. They have been living with her parents since they were married. _____

7. He has worked for that firm since 1997._____

8. I have not seen her since last week._____

9. The dog hasn't eaten anything since Wednesday. _____

10. They haven't sent him any money since last summer. _____

Yet means so far; it is used in negatives and questions.

Sean hasn't called *yet*.	**Has Sean called *yet*?**

Already means *by this time* or *previously*; it is used in affirmative statements and questions.

They have *already* left.	**Have they *already* left?**

Practice

A *Complete the following sentences with* yet *or* already *as required by meaning.*

1. Martha hasn't called us ____yet____.

2. They have _____ mailed the check.

3. Is it time for us to leave _____? No, not _____.

4. Sal has _____ bought the tickets for the game.

5. We have _____ signed the contract.

6. We have _____ been to Mexico three times.

7. But you haven't visited Taxco _____.

8. Has Jim gotten his new car _____?

9. Has the meeting begun _____? No, not _____.

10. Have the police found the thief _____?

11. They haven't even started to look for him _____.

12. The plane has _____ left the airport.

B *Give a negative answer with* yet *to the following questions.*

1. Has Mel left yet? *No, Mel hasn't left yet.* _____

2. Has the mail arrived yet? _____

3. Have you finished your homework yet? _____

4. Has Mr. Dole returned from lunch yet? _____

5. Have you paid that bill yet? _____

6. Has the meeting begun yet? _____

7. Has George found a job yet? _____

8. Has the boat sailed yet? _____

9. Have you bought the tickets for the game yet? _____

10. Have you ridden in Pam's new car yet? _____

C *Give an affirmative answer with* already *to the questions in Exercise B.*

Has Mel left yet? *Yes, Mel has already left.* _____

SAY, TELL

Use the verb *say* for direct quotations.

> Maryanne *said*, "I am very busy."
>
> Yale *said* to me, "I don't feel well."

Use the verb *say* for indirect quotations when the person to whom the words are spoken is not mentioned.

> Maryanne *said* that she was very busy.

Use *say to* or *tell* for indirect quotations when the person to whom the words are spoken is mentioned.

> Bill *said* to his boss that he needed to leave early.
>
> Christine *told* me that she didn't feel well.

Note these idiomatic uses of the verb *tell*:

to tell a lie	to tell the truth	to tell time	tell apart
to tell a story	to tell a secret	to tell about something	

Practice

A *Supply the correct form of* say *or* tell *in these sentences.*

1. Carol ___*said*___ that she was going to Saratoga for the weekend.

2. Carol _____ me that she was going to Saratoga for the weekend.

3. I _____ my boss that I could not finish my work in time.

4. Paul _____ me all about his trip. He _____ it was exhausting.

5. Please _____ me about the movie that you saw last night. Ruth _____ that she liked it very much.

6. Grace _____ to me, "I shall never speak to him again."

7. I _____ William that I could not go to the movies with him.

8. The boy _____ his mother a lie, and she punished him severely. I believe he will always _____ the truth in the future.

9. The teacher _____ us that she was too busy to see us after class.

10. These twin brothers look so much alike that I cannot _____them apart.

11. Mr. and Mrs. Sula _____ us all about their recent trip to Japan. They _____ Japan was a very interesting and picturesque country.

12. William _____ to me, "Is it necessary to write all my papers in ink?"

13. _____ me just what you _____ yesterday about your vacation plans. He _____ that he wanted to go with you.

14. James always _____ the truth because his parents have trained him never to _____a lie.

15. Chan _____ she was too tired to go to the park with us.

16. The teacher _____ the class that she was not satisfied with their work.

17. My boss_____ me that I could take my vacation in July.

18. Can you _____ me how I can reach Pennsylvania Station?

19. Fred _____ English is difficult for him.

20. I have _____ him the same thing several times.

21. William _____ that the book belonged to Ms. Manley.

22. I _____ him that I thought it belonged to Patrick.

23. As part of his speech, the president _____ the audience several funny stories.

24. It was Kay who _____ us the secret of her success.

25. Will you please _____ me what time it is?

26. Who _____ you that Mr. Reese was a former army officer?

B) *Change these sentences to introduce* tell *in place of* say. *Then make whatever other changes are necessary.*

1. He said that he did not feel well. *He told me that he did not feel well.*

2. Gene said that he could not attend the meeting. _____

3. She said that she had a bad headache. _____

4. Joseph said that he was too busy to see us. _____

5. George said that he didn't have enough money to buy the tickets. _____

6. I said that I was going to buy the tickets. _____

7. The student said that he didn't know the meaning of many words in the lesson. _____

8. The man said that there were plenty of seats available. _____

9. The stockbroker said that he expected to make a lot of money. _____

10. The man said that he was German by birth. _____

11. He also said that he was a good friend of Lolita's. _____

12. Jean said that she had a lot of work to do. _____

C *Change these sentences to introduce* say *instead of* tell. *Then make whatever other changes are necessary.*

1. He told us that he was too tired to go out. *He said that he was too tired to go out.*

2. She told us that she knew how to speak French well. _____

3. I told him that I was too busy to see him. _____

4. We told him that there were many things worse than loss of hearing. _____

5. The manager told us that she was not satisfied with our work. _____

6. The doctor told me that I must rest more. _____

7. He told me that he knew her well. _____

8. I told the children that they should not make so much noise. _____

9. We told them that the train was late. _____

10. I told him that it was useless to wait any longer. _____

11. He told the girls that he was not married. _____

12. I told the teacher that I enjoyed the lesson very much. _____

Form the past perfect tense with *had* and the past participle of the main verb.

I had gone	we had gone
you had gone	you had gone
he had gone	
she had gone	they had gone
it had gone	

The past perfect tense describes an action that took place in the past before another past action. It is often used in conjunction with the past tense.

> By the time we arrived, they *had* already gone.
>
> Gertrude said that she *had seen* that movie before.

Practice

Supply the past perfect tense form of the verbs in parentheses.

1. Fernando told us that he ___had looked___ (look) everywhere for the book.

2. Carla _____ (leave) by the time we arrived.

3. The police reported that they finally _____ (capture) the thief.

4. I met them before I _____ (go) a hundred yards.

5. I saw that we _____ (take) the wrong road.

6. He knew that he _____ (make) a serious mistake.

7. I felt that I _____ (meet) the man somewhere before.

8. He asked me why I _____ (leave) the party so early.

9. He wanted to know what _____ (happen) to his briefcase.

10. Previously she _____ (be) a very good manager.

11. It was clear that he _____ (give) us the wrong address.

12. The teacher corrected the reports which I _____ (prepare).

13. What did he say she _____ (do) with the money?

14. He said he _____ (have) his lunch.

15. I was sure that I _____ (see) the man before.

As. . . as expresses equality of comparison. The phrase may be used with both adjectives and adverbs and in both positive and negative sentences. Negative sentences can also use so . . . as.

She is as tall as he.	She is not as tall as he.	She is not so tall as he.
He is as old as I.	He is not as old as I.	He is not so old as I.
She works as hard as he.	She does not work as hard as he.	She does not work so hard as he.
He can run as fast as I can.	He cannot run as fast as I can.	He cannot run so fast as I can.

Practice

Supply the phrase as . . . as *or* not so . . . as. *Also change all adjectives to their corresponding adverb forms where necessary.*

1. Reggie is ___as___ (tall) ___as___ his brother.
2. Our apartment is _____ (large) _____ yours.
3. This street is _____ (wide) _____ Broadway.
4. Stephen is not _____ (intelligent) _____ his sister.
5. I don't get up every morning _____ (early) _____ my parents.
6. She sings _____ (beautiful) _____ she plays.
7. We came _____ (quick) _____ we could.
8. We drove there _____ (fast) _____ we could.
9. He doesn't speak English _____ (good) _____ his sister.
10. Helen doesn't prepare her homework _____ (careful) _____ she should.
11. He doesn't attend class _____ (regular) _____ he should.
12. He didn't arrive _____ (early) _____ we expected.
13. Sharon can do the work _____ (easy) _____ I.
14. He doesn't work _____ (hard) _____ the other employees.
15. I came _____ (soon) _____ possible.
16. I don't believe that it is _____ (cold) today _____ it was yesterday.
17. Her pronunciation is not _____ (good) _____ yours.
18. We visit them _____ (often) _____ we can.

If the main verb of a sentence is in the past tense, all other dependent verbs are usually in the past tense too.

> I *think* I *need* more time.
>
> I *thought* I *needed* more time.
>
> He *says* he *will* bring the money tomorrow.
>
> He *said* he *would* bring the money tomorrow.
>
> She *thinks* John *is* working downtown.
>
> She *thought* John *was* working downtown.
>
> They *say* they *have* known her for a long time.
>
> They *said* they *had known* her for a long time.

Note the irregular past tense forms of the following modals:

will	would
can	could
may	might

Practice

 Change each of the following sentences to past time.

1. The newspaper says the President will arrive in the morning. *The newspaper said the President would arrive in the morning.*

2. She says she cannot do this work. _____

3. She says her name is Smith. _____

4. I think I can finish this report by five o'clock. _____

5. The meteorologist predicts that it will rain tomorrow. _____

6. Mr. Wik says he is very busy. _____

7. She complains that she has a headache. _____

8. He thinks he may finish his work by two o'clock. _____

9. I do not think I can complete this report on schedule. _____

10. He promises that the error will not occur again. _____

11. He says the mail will certainly be here by noon. _____

12. The students think they are making sufficient progress. _____

13. They say the weather will probably be cold next week. _____

14. I think it will rain today. _____

15. He hopes he can get there on time. _____

16. I don't think I will see you again. _____

17. She says she may be late. _____

18. I think he is out of town. _____

19. Does she say he can't do it? _____

20. He complains that nobody believes a word he says. _____

21. I am certain that the price will go up soon. _____

22. She tells me that prices are sure to rise. _____

23. He promises faithfully that he will deliver the goods. _____

24. He hopes he may reach home before night. _____

25. He says that he has known her for many years. _____

26. She says she has lived here three years. _____

27. She thinks she can get here by noon. _____

28. He says he is taking English lessons from Ms. Campbell. _____

29. The jury declares that the prisoner isn't guilty. _____

30. They feel sure the battle will be over before tomorrow. _____

31. I wonder what changes the new chairman will introduce. _____

32. He swears he has never seen the man before. _____

B *Change the following sentences from the past tense to the present tense.*

1. He said he would leave in the morning. *He says he will leave in the morning.*

2. They thought they had found the thief, but they were mistaken. _____

3. He thought the mail would surely be here by noon. _____

4. The paper said it would rain today. _____

5. She said her name was Garcia. _____

6. He said that he was too busy to come to class. _____

7. I did not think he could finish that report today. _____

8. He said he'd be here by noon. _____

9. I did not think she'd come. _____

10. Did he say he'd call again? _____

11. She promised she'd try to do better work. _____

12. He told me he thought prices were going up. _____

13. He said he had found the book. _____

14. She said she couldn't understand what I meant. _____

May indicates possible future action.

> **He *may* leave tomorrow. (He hasn't decided yet.)**

___

Practice

 A *Change each of these sentences to introduce* may.

1. It is possible that he'll return later. *He may return later.*

2. Perhaps she'll help us with this work. *She may help us with this work.*

3. It is possible Len will be at the meeting tonight. _____

4. Perhaps Loretta will lend us the money. _____

5. Perhaps she will call you later. _____

6. Possibly Frank will offer to lend his car. _____

7. Possibly the weather will get warmer tomorrow. _____

8. It is possible that she is sick. _____

9. It is possible you will feel better later. _____

10. Perhaps it will not rain this afternoon. _____

11. It is possible that we shall be late for the meeting. _____

12. Perhaps he will not want to go with us. _____

13. Possibly they will go by plane. _____

14. Perhaps they will go to South America instead of to Europe on their vacation. _____

B *Answer each of these questions using* may. *Also add* I'm not sure *at the end of your answer.*

1. Will Lois help us with the work? *She may help us with the work. I'm not sure.*

2. Will Ian pass all his examinations? _____

3. Will David be back by noon? _____

4. Will Mary drive us to the beach? _____

5. Are you going to the movies tonight? _____

6. Are you going to Europe on your vacation? _____

7. Will Nell wait for us after the lesson?_____

8. Will you see Liz tomorrow? _____

9. Will Fran lend us the money which we need? _____

10. Are the Kleins going to take the children with them to Toronto?_____

SHOULD, OUGHT TO

Should and *ought to* are used to express advisability. They have the same meaning and can be used interchangeably. The contraction *shouldn't* is commonly used.

> Albert *should spend* more time studying.
>
> Albert *ought to spend* more time studying.
>
> You *shouldn't smoke* so much. You *should not smoke* so much.
>
> You *ought not to smoke* so much.

Practice

A *Complete the following sentences with* should. *In negative sentences, use the contracted form.*

1. She ___should try___ (try) to finish her projects on time.

2. They _____ not (make) so much noise.

3. I _____ (spend) more time on my English.

4. He _____ not (eat) so much.

5. You _____ (learn) as many new words as possible.

6. You _____ (ask) permission before doing it.

7. He _____ (get) more physical exercise.

8. You really _____ (go) to see a doctor.

9. Someone _____ (tell) him all about it.

10. No one _____ (spend) as much money as she does.

11. She _____ not (waste) so much time on unimportant details.

12. I _____ (write) them a letter, but I don't have anything to say.

13. You _____ not (work) so hard.

14. You _____ (rest) more and try to build up your strength.

15. We _____ (pay) more attention to what the teacher says.

B *Complete the sentences in Exercise A with* ought to.

She ___ought to try___ (try) to finish her projects on time.

Have to and *must* express necessity or strong obligation. *Have to* is the more commonly used term.

You *must* go home.	You *have to* go home.
Linda *must* work tonight.	Linda *has to* work tonight.

Practice

Substitute the correct form of have to *for* must *in the following sentences.*

1. He must leave at once. *He has to leave at once.*_____

2. They must stay there at least an hour. _____

3. You must mail that package today._____

4. He must have more practice in conversation. _____

5. They must help her with that work. _____

6. You must speak to him about it today._____

7. He must spend more time on his homework. _____

8. You must write them a letter. _____

9. We must leave before Helen gets here. _____

10. We must learn at least ten new words every day._____

11. I must take this package to the post office._____

12. You must insure it. _____

13. Roger must give you a receipt. _____

14. They must spend more time on their English._____

15. You must pay more attention to pronunciation. _____

16. You must help her in every way possible. _____

HAVE TO

Past, Future, and Present Perfect Forms

Use *have to,* not *must,* to express obligation or necessity in the past, future, and present perfect tenses.

> I *had to* work last night.
>
> I *will have to* work tomorrow.
>
> I *have had to* work every night this week.

Practice

A *Change* have to *to the past tense in these sentences.*

1. He has to get up early. *He had to get up early.*

2. She has to have more money. _____

3. Boris has to have an interpreter with him at all times. _____

4. Everyone has to work overtime. _____

5. He has to learn English quickly. _____

6. I have to go to the post office. _____

7. She has to return later. _____

8. He has to see the doctor a second time. _____

9. We have to lend him some money. _____

10. You have to spend more time on your homework. _____

11. They have to leave for New York immediately. _____

12. We have to stay there all summer. _____

13. You have to send it by air express. _____

14. He has to give me a receipt. _____

B *Change* have to *in the sentences in Exercise A to the future tense. Add any words which may be necessary to complete the meaning.*

He has to get up early. *He'll have to get up early if he wants to be there on time.*

Negatives and Questions

Use the negative form of *have to* to express lack of obligation or necessity. Form negatives with *have to* by placing *do not, does not, did not,* or *will not* before *have*. The contracted forms *don't, doesn't, didn't,* and *won't* are generally used.

Herb *has to* work tonight.	Herb *doesn't have to* work tonight.
She'll *have to* pay by check.	She *won't have to* pay by check.

Form questions with *have to* by placing *do, does, did* or *will* before the subject.

Herb *has to* work tonight.	**Does** Herb *have to* work tonight?
She'll *have to* pay by check.	**Will** she *have to* pay by check?

Practice

A *Change the following sentences from affirmative to negative.*

1. The nurse had to work in the Recovery Room. *The nurse didn't have to work in the Recovery Room.*

2. They'll have to buy their tickets early. _____

3. I have to cash this check today. _____

4. He had to pay the doctor before leaving the office. _____

5. They had to go by train. _____

6. She has to take a make-up examination. _____

7. He has to write many business letters. _____

8. We'll have to take an earlier flight. _____

9. They had to wait a long time for an answer to their letter. _____

10. They have to learn many new words every day. _____

11. I have to go to the dentist again next week. _____

12. We had to wait in his office a long time. _____

B *Change the sentences in Exercise A to questions.*

The nurse had to work in the Recovery Room. *Did the nurse have to work in the Recovery Room?*

Information Questions

Form information questions with *have to* by placing *do, does, did,* or *will* before the subject and adding a question word.

> **How long will** we *have* to wait for the package?

Practice

Change the following sentences to questions beginning with the question words in parentheses.

1. He had to leave at six o'clock. (What time) *What time did he have to leave?*

2. They had to wait there for two hours. (How long) _____

3. The children had to stay indoors because it was raining. (Why) _____

4. They had to leave the party early because Jay was sick. (Why) _____

5. He has to go to Denver on Sunday. (When) _____

6. He will have to stay there for a month. (How long) _____

7. They had to pay $15 for their medicine. (How much) _____

8. I have to go to the dentist again next week. (When) _____

9. You will have to come back at five o'clock. (What time) _____

10. He has to go to the post office to buy some stamps. (Why) _____

11. Each student has to learn ten new words every day. (How many new words) _____

12. She has to go there twice a week. (How often) _____

13. They had to leave $20 as a deposit. (How much) _____

14. He has to leave at three o'clock. (What time) _____

15. You have to sign your name at the bottom of the page. (Where) _____

16. Mary has to do all the housework now because her husband is ill. (Why) _____

17. I'll have to ask my parents for the money. (Whom) _____

A preposition is used before a noun, pronoun, or gerund to show place, time, or direction. Prepositions include:

about	behind	into	toward
above	below	near	under
across	beside	of	until
after	between	off	up
against	by	on	upon
along	down	out	with
among	during	over	within
around	for	since	
at	from	through	
before	in	to	

Practice

 A *Supply the correct prepositions for the following sentences.*

1. This book belongs ____to____ Theodore.

2. We all went _____ a walk _____ the park.

3. We bought this car _____ August.

4. We plan to trade it _____ a new one _____ the spring.

5. We looked everywhere _____ the pen which Guy lost.

6. Nan usually sits _____ this desk.

7. I make a lot of errors _____ spelling.

8. The man walked quickly _____ the room and sat down.

9. She spends a lot _____ time _____ her English.

10. We read _____ the accident _____ the newspaper this morning.

11. I must write a letter _____ my aunt.

12. She went _____ the corner store _____ some groceries.

13. Lea sits _____ front _____ me at the meeting.

14. The boat moved slowly _____ the coast.

15. Everyone laughed _____ William's story.

16. The woman smiled _____ me pleasantly.

17. He thanked me _____ my interest _____ the matter.

18. How much did they pay _____ their new home?

19. They buy everything _____ credit.

20. They told me all _____ their trip _____ South America.

21. He left the office _____ once, as soon as he heard _____ the accident.

22. Please put those papers _____ that drawer.

B *Supply the correct prepositions for the following sentences.*

1. She almost got run over when she walked in front ____*of*____ a fast-moving car.

2. The book is _____ the desk.

3. He walked _____ the room.

4. He looked _____ the window.

5. I put the letter _____ his hands.

6. The ship is now five miles _____ the port.

7. The Rocky Mountains are west _____ the Mississippi River.

8. Heat changes ice _____ water.

9. Sit _____ that chair.

10. Do you usually have dinner _____ home or _____ a restaurant?

11. He arrived _____ Hawaii _____ five o'clock.

12. Our office is six blocks _____ the station.

13. I heard it _____ the radio.

14. We stopped overnight _____ Pittsburgh.

15. Wait for us _____ the corner _____ 36th Street.

16. I'll meet you _____ front _____ the building.

17. Shelly sat here _____ me.

18. He arrived _____ five o'clock _____ a taxi.

19. The wind blew the paper _____ the window.

20. The dog jumped _____ the fence.

21. I saw him _____ the corner _____ Broadway and 42nd Street.

22. The ball rolled _____ the table _____ the floor.

23. He walked quickly _____ the door.

24. He sat down _____ the table and began to write _____ his notebook.

25. We walked _____ the street and looked _____ all the shop windows.

C *Supply the correct prepositions for the following sentences.*

1. I won't be back ____*for*____ several hours. You should eat __*without*__ me.

2. Everyone had finished dinner _____ ten o'clock.

3. Will you lend me your pen _____ a few minutes?

4. It has been raining steadily _____ yesterday.

5. I have known Daphne _____ many years.

6. France has been a republic _____ 1871.

7. I will wait for him _____ three o'clock.

8. The game lasted _____ three hours.

9. Yesterday I bought a new tie _____ Ivy's. _____ the same time, I bought a new shirt.

10. I did not finish my work _____ time to show it _____ the teacher.

11. I have been working on this _____ an hour.

12. I get up _____ seven o'clock every morning and go to bed _____ twelve.

13. I told him I would be there _____ an hour.

14. I am usually quite tired _____ the end _____ the day.

15. His health is improving day _____ day.

16. I see him _____ time _____ time.

17. Once _____ awhile I walk _____ work.

18. His office hours are _____ nine _____ five.

19. Did anyone call me _____ my absence?

20. Al arrived _____ seven o'clock sharp.

21. The train will leave _____ five minutes.

22. He didn't arrive until late _____ the afternoon.

23. I get up _____ six o'clock and have my breakfast _____ seven.

24. I have not been there _____ last summer.

D *Supply the correct prepositions for the following sentences.*

1. I usually come to work ____*by*____ subway.

2. I will do that _____ pleasure.

3. He spoke _____ a low voice.

4. The car was traveling _____ full speed.

5. Shall we go _____ the bus or _____ a cab?

6. I am sorry, but I don't agree _____ you.

7. She is afraid _____ animals.

8. The messenger has just left a box of flowers _____ you.

9. He was _____ a hurry.

10. The plane flew directly _____ our house.

11. He is going to ask Grace _____ a date.

12. Some workers are paid _____ the day, others _____ the week.

13. There is something wrong _____ this telephone.

14. Please write your signature _____ ink.

15. _____ the way, have you seen Elvira lately?

16. I went there _____ mistake.

17. Bill and Gina fell _____ love _____ each other.

18. Slowly the airplane came _____ sight.

19. It is dark here. Please turn _____ the light.

20. They are both very fond _____ music.

21. There is not enough room _____ all of us.

22. I explained _____ him that the elevator was out _____ order.

23. This is an exception _____ the rule.

24. It will be impossible _____ me to go _____ you _____ the theater.

25. There is a great difference _____ that book and this one.

The passive voice shows that the subject is receiving the action of the verb. Form the passive voice by using the appropriate form of *to be* and the past participle of the main verb.

Tense	Active Voice	Passive Voice
Present	Amy writes a letter.	A letter *is written* by Amy.
Past	Amy wrote a letter.	A letter *was written* by Amy.
Future	Amy will write a letter.	A letter *will be written* by Amy.
Present Perfect	Amy has written a letter.	A letter *has been written* by Amy.

Practice

 A *Change the following sentences from the active voice to the passive voice. Be sure to keep the same tense.*

1. Wayne delivers the mail every day. <u>*The mail is delivered by Wayne every day.*</u>

2. Fire destroyed that house. _____

3. The audience enjoyed the concert very much. _____

4. Bob took that book from the desk._____

5. Walter will eat the cake. _____

6. Beth has finished the report. _____

7. Ms. Duke will leave the tickets at the box office. _____

8. The messenger has just left a box of flowers for you. _____

9. The police easily captured the thief. _____

10. Many people attended the lecture. _____

11. The movie disappointed us very much. _____

12. Mr. Jones manages the export division._____

13. John returned the money last night._____

B *Change the following sentences from the passive voice to the active voice. Be sure to keep the same tense.*

1. That book was written by Andy Murphy. <u>*Andy Murphy wrote that book.*</u>

2. The entire city was destroyed by the fire. _____

3. The town was captured by the enemy._____

4. The money has been stolen from my purse by someone. _____

5. The book was found by Mary. _____

6. The book has been returned by John. _____

7. The book is read by many people all over the world. _____

8. The mail is delivered by Paula. _____

C *Change the following sentences from active to passive. Do not change the tense.*

1. The teacher corrects our exercises at home. *Our exercises are corrected at home by the teacher.*

2. They started a dancing class last week. _____

3. Mr. Smith saw the accident. _____

4. He left the report on the desk. _____

5. Everybody will see this film soon. _____

6. He has just finished the report. _____

7. An economic crisis followed the war. _____

8. Somebody has taken my briefcase. _____

9. The teacher returned our written work to us. _____

10. Valerie buys books from that store. _____

11. She had finished the report by noon. _____

12. The mad dog bit the little boy. _____

13. The wind blows the fog away by midmorning. _____

14. The committee will choose you as its representative. _____

15. The maid broke the plate and the glass. _____

16. Tall trees lined the street. _____

17. The newspapers reported the event immediately. _____

18. We heard the sound of music. _____

19. The police have arrested five suspects. _____

20. The neighborhood children played with our dog. _____

21. The doctor ordered him to take a long rest. _____

22. Lightning struck the house. _____

Form the passive voice of *can, have to, may, must, ought to,* and *should* with *be* and the past participle of the main verb.

I *have to* finish this work.	This work *has to be finished.*
You *can* see it now.	It *can be seen by* you now.
He *should* type his term paper.	His term paper *should be typed.*

Form the passive voice in the continuous tenses with *being* and the past participle of the main verb.

She *is climbing* the mountain.	The mountain *is being climbed* by her.

Practice

Change the following sentences from the active to the passive voice.

1. We may finish the leftovers in the refrigerator. *The leftovers in the refrigerator may be finished.*

2. They should send it to us at once. _____

3. The mailman is delivering the mail now. _____

4. He has to finish it today. _____

5. The police are holding him for further questioning. _____

6. They may organize a new group next week. _____

7. You ought to write that letter today. _____

8. The citizens are defending the city bravely. _____

9. They cannot hold the meeting in that room. _____

10. They may deliver the merchandise while we are out. _____

11. He has to pay the bill before the first of the month. _____

12. He may pay the bill for us. _____

13. Congress is debating that question today. _____

14. For the time being, Karen is teaching that group. _____

15. You ought to water the plant once a week. _____

16. The company is shipping the merchandise today. _____

17. We must warn them of the danger. _____

Negatives and Questions

Form negatives in the passive voice by placing *not* after the auxiliary verb. The contracted forms are often used.

> **The film *was not directed* by Steven Spielberg.**
>
> **The bricks *won't be delivered* before Tuesday.**

Form questions in the passive voice by placing the auxiliary verb before the subject.

> ***Was* the film *directed* by Steven Spielberg?**
>
> ***Will* the bricks *be delivered* before Tuesday?**

Add a question word to form information questions.

> ***When will* the prize *be awarded?***

Practice

 A *Change the following sentences from affirmative to negative. Use the full form and the contracted form.*

1. He was sent to Los Angeles. _He was not sent to Los Angeles. He wasn't sent to Los Angeles._

2. This must be finished today. _____

3. The letter has already been sent. _____

4. The book was published in 1982. _____

5. The class is taught by Ms. Smith. _____

6. The merchandise is being sent today. _____

7. The thief has been caught by the police. _____

8. The fire was started by an arsonist. _____

9. The chairs have been put in Room 10. _____

10. The jewels were stolen by one of the servants. _____

11. The book will be published in the spring. _____

12. The lecture was attended by many people. _____

13. The first prize was won by Maria. _____

14. The accident was caused by Vance's carelessness. _____

15. Our exercises will be corrected each night. _____

16. The house was completely destroyed by the fire. _____

17. The tickets have been purchased. _____

18. The bridge was designed by a French architect. _____

B *Change the sentences in Exercise A to questions.*

He was sent to Los Angeles. *Was he sent to Los Angeles?* _____

C *Change the following sentences to questions beginning with the question word in parentheses.*

1. The house was built in 1975. (When) *When was the house built?* _____

2. The building was destroyed by fire. (How) _____

3. The merchandise will be delivered next week. (When) _____

4. The money had been stolen by the workers. (Who) _____

5. The child was finally found in the park. (Where) _____

6. He was injured in an airplane accident. (What) _____

7. The mail is delivered at ten o'clock. (When) _____

8. The contract must be signed by Mr. Smith. (Who) _____

9. The tickets will be left at the box office. (Where) _____

10. San Francisco was nearly destroyed by earthquake in 1906. (When) _____

11. The book was published in France. (Where) _____

12. He was operated on for appendicitis. (What) _____

13. The boy was punished because he had run away. (Why) _____

14. The note was left on the table. (Where) _____

15. The city was captured by the enemy in June. (When) _____

16. The money was put into the safe. (Where) _____

17. The bridge will be finished this year. (When) _____

18. It was designed by a French engineer. (Who) _____

SUPPOSED TO

Supposed to used with the simple form of the main verb expresses anticipation or expectation. This term has a present and a past tense.

> **Ms. Garcia *is supposed to* be here. (Present)**
>
> **We *were supposed to* arrive last night, but we were delayed. (Past)**

Practice

Supply the correct form of (to be) supposed to.

1. Doris and I *were supposed to send* (send) the plans last night.

2. The ship _____ (sail) two hours ago.

3. She _____ (come) at four o'clock yesterday afternoon.

4. He _____ (be) here now.

5. Lilly _____ (bring) the books with her.

6. That letter _____ (write) yesterday.

7. I _____ (mail) this package last Saturday.

8. He _____ (leave) for Europe next week, but he may have to postpone his trip until next month.

9. He _____ (take) his lesson at ten o'clock, but we haven't seen him.

10. Which room is the club _____ (meet) in?

11. Next week, the bridge club _____ (meet) in Room 10, but the other club _____ (meet) on the tenth floor.

12. Which line am I _____ (write) my name on?

13. I'm sorry that I must leave so soon, but I _____ (be) at the consulate at twelve o'clock.

14. Ann wants to know whether she _____ (take) her pill at ten o'clock or twelve o'clock.

15. The catalogue _____ (publish) next spring.

Used to describes an action that was customary or that happened for some time in the past but that does not happen at the present time.

> **We lived in Maryland before we moved here.**
>
> **We *used to* live in Maryland.**

> **I taught English for years; now I'm retired.**
>
> **I *used to* teach English.**

Used to is followed by the simple form of the verb.

___

Practice

In each of the following sentences, change the italicized verb to introduce used to.

1. I *walked* to work. *I used to walk to work.* _____
2. I never *made* so many mistakes in spelling. _____
3. The accounting department *was* on the 18th floor. _____
4. Tom *was* a good employee and *worked* hard. _____
5. I *bought* all my clothes in that store. _____
6. This building *was* occupied by a large insurance firm. _____
7. Betty *had* charge of the transportation division. _____
8. Gary *played* the violin. _____
9. Laura *went* to the concert every week. _____
10. He never *did* his work poorly. _____
11. He *took* a great interest in his piano lessons. _____
12. All meetings *were* held in the auditorium. _____
13. Marcus *was* the official interpreter for the company. _____
14. I *used* my computer a great deal. _____
15. Mr. Earl *worked* in this office. _____
16. I never *caught* cold. _____
17. It *was* my custom to practice the piano every day. _____

Would rather followed by the simple form of the verb means *to prefer*. The contracted form *'d rather* is generally used. Note the position and use of *than*.

> I would *rather* watch TV *than* go to a movie.
>
> She'd *rather* walk *than* take a taxi.
>
> We'd *rather* go to the cabin this weekend. (An implied comparison with any other choice)

Practice

Change these sentences to introduce would rather. *Use both the full form and the contracted form. Be sure that* rather *appears only once in each clause.*

1. I prefer to wait outside rather than in here. *I would rather wait outside than in here.*
   I'd rather wait outside than in here.

2. They prefer to walk to school._____

3. We prefer to spend the summer at home instead of in the country. _____

4. The doctor says that he prefers to examine you in his office. _____

5. I prefer not to mention it to him at this time. _____

6. I prefer to eat at home rather than in a restaurant. _____

7. He prefers to meet us downtown._____

8. I prefer to speak with her in private. _____

9. I prefer to drive a small car rather than a big one. _____

10. Jean prefers to study in this class instead of in the advanced class._____

11. I prefer to do all my homework before I leave school. _____

12. He prefers to live in a large city like London._____

13. I prefer to live in a small town. _____

14. I prefer to work in my garden rather than play golf._____

15. I prefer to see a good movie rather than go to the opera. _____

16. He prefers to attend a large college; I prefer to go to a small one._____

Had better with the simple form of the verb means *it would be better* or *it would be advisable*. The contracted form *'d better* is generally used. Note that this term expresses a future thought even though it is in a past form.

> **You *had better* see a doctor.**   **You*'d better* see a doctor.**

Add *not* to form the negative.

> **They *had better not* forget their homework again.**

Practice

Change these sentences to introduce had better. *Use the full form and the contracted form.*

1. It would be better if you came back later. *You had better come back later.*
   You'd better come back later.

2. It would be better if she rested a while. _____

3. It would be better if Betty gave you back the money._____

4. It would be better if she didn't see him again. _____

5. It would be advisable for them to save their money. _____

6. It would be better if you didn't mention this to anyone. _____

7. It would be advisable for you to send an invitation._____

8. It would be better if you didn't tell Carmen about this. _____

9. It would be advisable for you to tell them the truth. _____

10. It would be better if Neil prepared his homework more carefully._____

11. It would be advisable for you not to drive so fast on this road._____

12. You shouldn't give them too much information. _____

13. You should notify the police at once. _____

14. I advise you to spend more time on your piano lessons. _____

TAG ENDINGS

Tag endings ask a question or invite confirmation of some fact we already know. Tag endings contain a pronoun and an auxiliary verb but not a main verb. Use a negative tag ending after an affirmative sentence.

> Cyril can speak English, *can't he?*
>
> She's an American, *isn't she?*
>
> You live in Virginia, *don't you?*
>
> They'll be at the party, *won't they?*

Practice

Add the correct tag ending to the following sentences.

1. She goes shopping every day, _doesn't she_?
2. He has been studying English a long time, _____?
3. Matthew is a good student, _____?
4. She plays the piano well, _____?
5. She can play the piano well, _____?
6. You played tennis yesterday, _____?
7. The traffic is heavy today, _____?
8. The traffic was also heavy yesterday, _____?
9. You always buy your clothes at a department store, _____?
10. They go for a walk in the park every Sunday, _____?
11. You'll be back before noon, _____?
12. You have read that book, _____?
13. They are very old friends, _____?
14. It takes more than an hour to get there, _____?
15. The bus stops at this corner, _____?
16. They are traveling in Quebec now, _____?
17. I gave you what you wanted, _____?
18. She was unkind to you, _____?
19. You could drive that truck, _____?

Use an affirmative tag ending after a negative sentence.

> **Carl can't speak English,** *can he?*
>
> **She isn't an American,** *is she?*
>
> **You don't live in Virginia,** *do you?*
>
> **They won't be at the party,** *will they?*

Practice

 A *Add the correct tag ending to the following sentences.*

1. Catherine doesn't like to study geometry, ___does she___?

2. You haven't ever been in South America, _____?

3. You won't mention this to anyone, _____?

4. The traffic today isn't very heavy, _____?

5. The traffic wasn't heavy yesterday either, _____?

6. They didn't go by plane, _____?

7. Beth didn't say anything to you about it, _____?

8. He wasn't driving fast at the time, _____?

9. She doesn't know how to dance, _____?

10. Joe won't be back before noon, _____?

11. The bus doesn't stop near here, _____?

12. You didn't write those letters, _____?

13. I haven't paid you yet, _____?

14. Helen isn't going with you, _____?

15. You haven't had your lunch yet, _____

16. He can't speak English, _____?

17. I shouldn't drive so fast on this road, _____?

18. We won't have enough money to get in, _____?

19. They wouldn't give you the information, _____?

B *Add the correct tag endings to these sentences.*

1. Gregory left class early today, ___*didn't he*___?

2. He is an excellent student, _____?

3. She has never gotten in touch with you, _____?

4. Today is Wednesday, _____?

5. You live in Minnesota, _____?

6. You were absent yesterday, _____?

7. Both men look very much alike, _____?

8. They don't know each other, _____?

9. This street runs north and south, _____?

10. We won't have to stand in line, _____?

11. You mailed that letter, _____?

12. You didn't forget to put a stamp on it, _____?

13. She can speak French well, _____?

14. He never comes to class on time, _____?

15. The train is supposed to arrive soon, _____?

16. This bus stops at the airport, _____?

17. She is making good progress in French, _____?

18. Your sister has been sick a long time, _____?

19. This is your umbrella, _____?

20. There is someone at the door, _____?

21. The telephone rang, _____?

22. They paid you what they owed you, _____?

23. You'll call me in the morning, _____?

24. It hasn't come true yet, _____?

25. My mother has spoken to you, _____?

C *Add tag endings to the following sentences.*

1. He speaks English well, ___*doesn't he*___?
2. She writes a lot of letters, _____?
3. He is a busy man, _____?
4. He makes a lot of mistakes in pronunciation, _____?
5. Steven spends a lot of money on clothes, _____?
6. He always comes to class on time, _____?
7. Tony is out of town, _____?
8. There are a lot of students absent from class, _____?
9. They are good friends, _____?
10. They watch television every night, _____?
11. You enjoy your computer science class, _____?
12. The mail is delivered at ten o'clock, _____?
13. You spend a lot of time with them, _____?
14. She has to work very hard, _____?
15. He is too old to play football, _____?
16. You have piano lessons twice a week, _____?
17. The plane arrives at noon, _____?
18. They visit you every Sunday, _____?
19. You get up early every morning, _____?
20. He sits in the front row, _____?
21. She works in the import department, _____?
22. He is a good salesman, _____?

D *Change the sentences in Exercise C to the past and add the tag endings.*

He spoke English well, ___*didn't he*___?

E *Change the sentences in Exercise C to the future with* will *and add the tag endings.*

He will speak English well, ___*won't he*___?

IT, THERE

The impersonal pronoun *it* is used in expressions of weather, time, and distance.

> **It is cold today.**   **It is ten o'clock.**
>
> **It is a long way from here to California.**

It is also used with the verb *to be,* an adjective, and an infinitive.

> **It is easy to learn English grammar.**
>
> **It was difficult to find your address.**

There is and *there are* are used to express the existence of an object or objects.

> **There is a fly in the room.**
>
> **There are twelve people on that jury.**

Practice

 A *Complete the following sentences with* It is *or* There is.

1. ___It is___ raining very hard.

2. _____ plenty of time to do that later.

3. _____ a strange man in Bertha's office.

4. _____ easy to understand why he is angry.

5. _____ time for you to take your medicine.

6. _____ almost ten o'clock.

7. _____ a new moon tonight.

8. _____ a cat in one of your flower beds.

9. _____ impossible to finish that work in such a short time.

10. _____ warm in this room.

11. _____ hard to hear the music from the back of the room.

12. _____ ten miles from here to the university.

13. _____ a mailbox on the corner.

14. _____ a long line of cars ahead of us.

130 Grammar Essentials

15. _____ important to continue studying English.

16. _____ a lot of static on our radio.

17. _____ easy to understand her accent.

B *Complete the following sentences with* It *or* There.

1. _____*It*_____ is raining very hard.

2. _____ is a letter for you on the hall table.

3. _____ is almost three o'clock.

4. _____ is very cold today.

5. _____ are several Germans in our English class.

6. _____ is very hot in this room.

7. _____ is difficult to speak English well.

8. _____ is not a cloud in the sky.

9. _____ is beginning to snow.

10. _____ is hard to learn English in such a short time.

11. _____ are a lot of beautiful homes on this street.

12. _____ is unfortunate that you can't come with us.

13. _____ was midnight when we got home.

14. _____ is no place like home.

15. _____ was nice to see you.

16. _____ is a long way from here to Honolulu.

17. _____ are a lot of people in the park this afternoon.

18. _____ was almost eight o'clock when they arrived.

19. _____ were a lot of employees absent today.

20. _____ is Tuesday.

21. _____ is someone at the door.

22. _____ is very unpleasant to work in this cold room.

23. _____ is dangerous to drive so fast.

24. _____ are only twenty-eight days in February.

IT, THERE

C *Change the following sentences so that each one begins with* It.

1. Learning English is not easy. *It is not easy to learn English.* _____

2. Learning new words every day is important. _____

3. Studying with Mr. Nathan is very rewarding. _____

4. To pay so much money for a car that is old is foolish. _____

5. To drive so fast is dangerous. _____

6. Traveling in foreign countries is interesting. _____

7. To be able to speak a foreign language is often helpful. _____

8. To blame Rocky for that mistake is unfair. _____

9. Studying grammar is not interesting for a lot of students. _____

10. Understanding grammar is important. _____

11. Getting up early in the morning is almost impossible for me. _____

12. Going by bus is faster than going by car. _____

13. To sing in such a low key is not easy for a soprano. _____

14. To explain this matter to him will be difficult. _____

15. Working twelve hours a day at your age is foolish. _____

16. Spending the afternoon at the beach will be pleasant. _____

17. To call her at this late hour would be unwise. _____

18. Eating quickly is not satisfying. _____

19. Accepting their apologies is not easy. _____

20. Being comfortable in such hot weather is difficult. _____

21. Competing for the top prize is not easy. _____

D *Change the following sentences so that each one begins with* There is *or* There are.

1. A new magazine is on the hall table. *There is a new magazine on the hall table.* _____

2. A lot of trees are in the park. _____

3. Two strange men are in the living room. _____

4. Several people are waiting to see Dr. Quarles. _____

5. A letter for you is in the mailbox. _____

6. A storm is approaching. _____

7. A lot of dark clouds are in the sky. _____

8. Two policemen are on the corner. _____

9. A dog is in the garden. _____

10. Two children are playing on your front lawn. _____

11. Only one window is in the room. _____

12. Two tall trees are in front of the house. _____

13. A blackboard is in every room. _____

14. Several pictures are on the wall of each room. _____

15. A lot of birds of various colors are in the trees. _____

16. A vase of flowers is on the table. _____

17. An inch of snow is on the ground. _____

18. Curtains are on each window. _____

19. A lot of interesting people are in my English class. _____

20. A mailbox is on the corner. _____

21. The report is on his desk. _____

22. Two tickets to the new show are waiting for you at the box office. _____

23. Some contracts are in his briefcase. _____

A gerund is a form of verb that functions as a noun and ends in *ing*. Certain verbs, like *enjoy, mind, stop, consider, appreciate,* and *finish* can be followed by gerunds but not infinitives.

> He *enjoys studying* English.
>
> I *finished reading* the lesson.
>
> He *has stopped trying* to be first.

Practice

In the sentences below, supply the gerund form of the verb shown in parentheses.

1. I am considering _____moving_____ (move) back to Montreal.

2. I enjoy _____ (study) with Ms. Kinsey.

3. Mr. Kent stopped _____ (go) to his English class.

4. Do you mind _____ (wait) a few minutes in the hall?

5. We are considering _____ (buy) a new computer.

6. Did you enjoy _____ (travel) through Canada last summer?

7. Ask that salesman whether he minds _____ (come) back this afternoon.

8. Mr. Lamb enjoys _____ (listen) to the radio.

9. Mr. and Mrs. Michaels have stopped _____ (use) their camcorder.

10. They resent _____ (hold) the classes in the evening instead of the morning.

11. We will avoid _____ (receive) visitors after 2:00 p.m.

12. They have finished _____ (paint) our apartment at last.

13. Paul was driving fast and couldn't avoid _____ (hit) the other car.

14. Joey denied _____ (take) the book.

15. You shouldn't risk _____ (go) out if you have a cold.

16. He admitted _____ (make) the mistake after we questioned him for a long time.

Gerunds may also be used after most prepositions but not after *to* when it is part of an infinitive.

> Jane is fond of *exercising*.
>
> We use this pot for *brewing* herb tea.

Gerunds are used after certain expressions, for example, *to be worth, no use,* and *to have fun.*

> The new Lucas film *is worth seeing*.
>
> It's *no use trying* to call them at this hour.
>
> Did you *have fun playing* soccer yesterday?

Practice

A *Supply the gerund form of the verb in parentheses.*

1. Were you successful in _____*seeing*_____ (see) Ms. Vaughn?

2. Is Kay fond of _____ (swim)?

3. He needs much more drill in _____ (spell).

4. There's no use _____ (call) Mr. Dennis. He's not at home now.

5. There is little chance of _____ (see) him today.

6. That salesman has left. He got tired of _____ (wait) for Ms. Moreno.

7. That book is well worth _____ (read).

8. We had fun _____ (visit) you last summer.

9. It is a question of _____ (find) the right person for the job.

10. Mr. Spock always takes great pleasure in _____ (help) others.

11. Do you think that lecture is worth _____ (attend)?

12. Mr. and Mrs. Johnson are thinking of _____ (move) to Colorado.

13. He insisted on _____ (help) me with the report.

14. May had fun _____ (dance) at the party.

15. Mr. Peters spoke this morning about _____ (start) a new class.

16. He has no intention of _____ (leave) the class at this time.

17. We are all looking forward to _____ (see) Ms. Robertson next week.

18. Is there any possibility of _____ (see) Mr. Black this morning?

GERUNDS

B *Using a gerund construction, complete the following sentences in your own words.*

1. She is not interested in *learning to speak English* _____.
2. We both enjoy _____.
3. We went straight home instead of _____.
4. I don't feel like _____.
5. He has no intention of _____.
6. Do you think that book is worth _____?
7. We congratulated him on _____.
8. Did you have fun _____?
9. He is tired of _____.
10. He left suddenly without _____.
11. Thank you for _____.
12. He insisted upon _____.
13. I can't imagine _____.
14. We are considering _____.
15. He says he doesn't feel like _____.
16. They have stopped _____.
17. There is little chance of _____.
18. He hasn't had any experience in _____.
19. You can't blame him for _____.
20. We all need more practice in _____.
21. We finally succeeded in _____.
22. They are thinking of _____.
23. They are both very fond of _____.
24. In the middle of our discussion, the man suddenly burst out _____.
25. Have you finished _____?
26. Mrs. Belkamp has suggested _____.
27. If we don't hurry, we'll miss _____.
28. The Cresseys had to postpone _____.
29. Did the prisoner escape _____?
30. Would you mind _____?

Certain verbs can be followed by either gerunds or infinitives. Some of these verbs are *start, begin, continue, like, neglect, hate, cease, love,* and *prefer.*

> **He has *begun to take* English lessons.**
>
> **He has *begun taking* English lessons.**

> **She will *continue to study* in that class.**
>
> **She will *continue studying* in that class.**

Practice

A *Complete each of the following sentences with a gerund.*

1. Micky prefers _____*taking*_____ (take) biology this semester.

2. He likes _____ (take) lessons from Miss Dixson.

3. I neglected _____ (tell) Mr. Hall about that report.

4. They prefer _____ (meet) at five o'clock instead of at six.

5. Joe will start _____ (work) in that department next week.

6. But he will continue _____ (take) frequent trips to the Midwest.

7. Meg loves _____ (work) for Mr. Harris.

8. He prefers _____ (leave) on the fifteenth.

9. He hates _____ (leave) the East Coast.

10. When will Mr. Hale start _____ (come) to class?

11. Ava likes _____ (study) in the fourth grade.

12. Mr. Hope prefers _____ (take) private lessons.

13. We hope to begin _____ (increase) our sales in the spring.

14. The enemies have continued _____ (build) up their armies.

15. Mary hates _____ (do) secretarial work.

B *Complete each of the sentences in Exercise A with an infinitive.*

Micky prefers _____*to take*_____ (take) biology this semester.

Form the future perfect tense with *will have* and the past participle of the main verb. The contracted form *'ll* is often used.

I will have worked	we will have worked	I'll/we'll have worked
you will have worked	you will have worked	you'll have worked
he/she/it will have worked	they will have worked	he'll/she'll/it'll/they'll have worked

The future perfect tense describes an action that will be a past and complete action at a certain point in the future.

> By next September I*'ll* have worked here thirty years.
>
> We will *have finished* this book in June.

Practice

Complete the following sentences with the future perfect tense form of the verbs in parentheses.

1. I am sure they <u>will have completed</u> (complete) the new road by June.

2. He says that before he leaves he _____ (see) every show in town.

3. If you don't make a note of that appointment, you _____ (forget) it by next week.

4. By this time next month, all the roses _____ (die).

5. By January first, all our work for the year _____ been _____ (finish) and our report _____ been _____ (turn) in.

6. By the time you arrive, I _____ (finish) reading your book.

7. I _____ (be) in this country for two years on January 12.

8. By this time next year, you _____ (forget) all your present troubles.

9. A century from now, wars, I hope, _____ (become) a thing of the past.

10. Perhaps by that time, we _____ (learn) that it is better to cooperate than to fight.

11. If he hasn't begun to study yet, he certainly _____ not _____ (learn) all his lessons by tomorrow.

12. I hope that by this time next year a peace treaty _____ been _____ (sign).

13. When you are my age, you _____ (learn) a lot.

14. A year from now he _____ (take) his medical exams and begun to practice.

Practice

A *Complete the following sentences with the correct tense of the verbs in parentheses.*

1. Daryl always _____comes_____ (come) to work on time.

2. Mr. Jones _____ (teach) us at present. He _____ (substitute) for Mr. Holt, who is our regular teacher.

3. I _____ (work) in my garden when you called me last night.

4. We _____ (take) our finals next week.

5. I _____ (come) to work on the bus this morning.

6. As I _____ (come) to work this morning, I _____ (meet) a boy who _____ (try) to sell me a watch.

7. I _____ (be) to the Grand Canyon several times.

8. Listen! I think the telephone _____ (ring).

9. Bob said that he _____ (see) that movie before.

10. I _____ (read) that novel three or four times.

11. By this time next year, we _____ (complete) all the exercises in this book.

12. The telephone _____ (ring) just as I _____ (leave) my house.

13. The sun _____ (shine) brightly when I got up this morning.

14. Our class _____ (begin) every morning at 8:30 and _____ (end) at 10:00.

15. We occasionally _____ (go) to the movies on Sunday.

16. Listen! Somebody _____ (knock) at the door.

17. Up to now, nothing _____(hear) from the search party.

18. Marjory, who is now in the fourth grade, _____ (study) English for three years.

19. Ruth _____ (study) French for a few months last year.

20. My brother-in-law _____ (come) to visit me next week.

B *Complete these sentences with the correct tense of the verbs in parentheses.*

1. The magician _____was doing_____ (do) tricks on the stage when we entered.

2. The newspaper says that the police in New Orleans finally _____ (catch) the bank robber.

3. Look! That child _____ (cross) the street against the light.

4. _____ she usually _____ (walk) along Spencer Street at the same time every morning?

5. She said that she _____ (leave) before she heard the news.

6. By this time next week, Rod and Alan _____ (visit) their grandmother.

7. By March 15, I _____ (be) here one year.

8. Deborah handed in the report which she _____ (write).

9. Lee usually _____ (study) very hard. In fact, whenever I _____ (see) him he _____ (study) something.

10. Have you any idea what she _____ (do) when I _____ (call) her tomorrow?

11. What _____ you _____ (do) when I called you last night?

12. Since when _____ Harry _____ (be) manager of this department?

13. He _____ (be) appointed last June and _____ (be) in charge ever since.

14. Where _____ you _____ (go) on your vacation next month?

15. He cooked the rabbit which he _____ (shoot) in the woods.

16. The sun _____ (shine) when I got up this morning, but by ten o'clock it _____ (disappear) behind the clouds.

17. The U.S. Civil War _____ (begin) in 1861 and it _____ (end) in 1865, but not before thousands of men _____ (lose) their lives.

C Complete these sentences with the correct tense of the verbs in parentheses.

1. Tod _____felt_____ (feel) refreshed by the lemonade he ___had drunk___ (drink) with us earlier.

2. Friends who _____ (tell) us the truth are often less appreciated than those who _____ (flatter) us.

3. What did you do when you discovered that you _____ (lose) your wallet?

4. While we _____ (drive) to Milwaukee, we _____ (have) two flat tires.

5. The minute the bell rang, the students _____ (jump) from their seats.

6. When we got home from work, we discovered that they _____ (come) and _____ (go.)

7. Ms. Sheldon _____ (trip) as she _____ (enter) the room.

8. Sidney _____ (choose) captain of the baseball team by the other players.

9. That movie _____ (see) by millions of people around the world.

10. Lilian noticed that we _____ (take) the wrong road.

11. My mother _____ (not see) well after dark, so she never _____ (drive) at night.

12. She _____ (not dance) for a long time because she _____ (break) her leg last month.

13. I _____ (go) to Greece on my last vacation.

14. Where _____ you_____ (go) on your last vacation?

15. Where _____ you _____ (go) on your next vacation?

16. Where _____ you usually _____ (go) on your vacations?

17. What _____ you _____ (do) right now?

Position

Place adverbs of time *(yesterday, last week, next month,* etc.) at the beginning or end of a sentence.

> I saw Ms. Anderson *yesterday.*
>
> *On Wednesday* you are due in court.

Place adverbs of frequency *(often, usually, generally, rarely, ever,* etc.) before the main verb except when the main verb is a form of *to be.*

> He *always* comes to class late.   She is *never* late for class.
>
> Does he *always* come to class late?   Is she *always* late for class?

Note that in sentences with auxiliary verbs, adverbs of frequency are after the auxiliary verbs but before the main verbs.

> He has *always* come late to class.
>
> We don't *usually* eat in the cafeteria.

Practice

Place the indicated adverb in the correct place in these sentences.

1. I saw Mr. Manchester in the cafeteria. (yesterday) *I saw Mr. Manchester in the cafeteria yesterday.*

2. Sam has been a very careful worker. (always)_____

3. He goes to Boston on business trips. (often) _____

4. He stays with me. (seldom)_____

5. We'll see you. (on Friday) _____

6. She played the piano. (last night) _____

7. He is planning to visit us at our home. (tonight)_____

8. She has spoken to me. (never) _____

9. Alice asks for help. (rarely) _____

10. Al is late for class. (always)_____

11. He has prepared his lessons. (always)_____

Position

12. We went for a walk in the park. (on Sunday) _____

13. We go for a walk in the park on Sunday. (usually) _____

14. Do you go for a walk on Sunday? (ever)_____

15. I go for a walk on Sunday. (never) _____

16. I spoke to Ellen about that matter. (on Tuesday) _____

17. He promised to give me an answer. (in the morning) _____

18. Have you visited Chicago? (ever) _____

19. Do you eat in the cafeteria? (usually)_____

20. Have you eaten in the cafeteria? (ever) _____

21. Have you finished writing your exercises? (yet) _____

22. I have spoken to him about that. (often) _____

23. Have you spoken to him about that? (ever)_____

24. Has he been late for his classes? (always) _____

25. I have been to Mt. Vernon, Washington's home. (never) _____

26. I have read that book. (twice) _____

27. I have read it. (never) Have you read it? (ever) _____

28. Mr. and Mrs. Smith visited their daughter in college. (last week) _____

29. He is too busy to eat lunch. (often) _____

30. He is leaving for Denver. (tomorrow) _____

31. Does she forget her key? (sometimes)_____

32. Does she get up early? (generally) _____

33. Has he been taller than his sister? (always) _____

34. Nobody has a bad word to say about Kay. (ever) _____

35. He will finish his work. (tomorrow)_____

36. He does his exercises carefully. (rarely)_____

37. Belinda is going to leave for California. (tomorrow) _____

38. I met him there. (yesterday) _____

Word order is very important in English sentences. The normal word order for an English statement is subject, verb, indirect object, direct object, adverbial modifiers. Be careful not to separate a verb and its direct object with an adverbial modifier.

| Wrong: | I saw *yesterday* my friend. |
| Correct: | I saw my friend *yesterday*. |

Practice

Reconstruct the following sentences and put them into good English form.

1. Jacob has been two years in this country. *Jacob has been in this country two years.*

2. He is studying now engineering at Columbia University. _____

3. He was so excited he well couldn't think. _____

4. The light was so bright that we had to cover from time to time our eyes. _____

5. She said that he had had already three operations. _____

6. I even didn't know that it was you who was calling me. _____

7. Throw me from the bus a kiss. _____

8. Karen went to see the mayor in a new skirt. _____

9. Louise comes sometimes to our house for the lesson, and I go sometimes to hers. _____

10. I used to like a lot the theater, but now I go every night to the movies. _____

11. Of course, always I speak German with my family and friends. _____

12. He is studying now French as well as English. _____

13. He has been two years here; perhaps it is more even than that. _____

14. It was so cold that summer that we had to wear now and then our overcoats. _____

15. I have every day to write a lot of letters in English. _____

16. He said that he had seen already that movie. _____

17. He comes seldom to the lesson on time. _____

18. Simon gave me this morning your message. _____

19. Please read slowly the whole sentence. _____

20. We went last night to the theater. _____

Still means *even up to the present time.* It indicates some continuing action. *Still* usually comes before the main verb.

> **He is *still* working in that office.**   **They *still* live in that house.**

Anymore indicates that an action that went on in the past has been discontinued. We usually place *anymore* at the end of a negative sentence.

> **He isn't working in that office *anymore*.**
>
> **They don't live in that house *anymore*.**

Practice

A *Complete the following sentences with* still *or* anymore.

1. He doesn't study in this class _anymore_ .

2. She is _____ working as a clerk in a department store.

3. He is _____ teaching geography in that same school.

4. Sue is _____ the best student in the class.

5. Ann is not the best student in the class _____.

6. We never see you at the school dances _____.

7. They don't live near us _____.

8. I seldom see George _____.

9. We are _____ good friends, although we rarely see each other.

10. Do they _____ spend each summer in Mexico City?

11. He _____ thinks that he is the best teacher in the department.

12. Dr. Jones is not our doctor _____.

13. I _____ think that Helen is the most interesting person in the whole school.

14. They are _____ bitter enemies, although they never see each other.

B *Change the following sentences from affirmative to negative.*

1. We are still good friends. _We are not good friends anymore._

2. He is still president of the club. _____

3. They still live on State Street. _____

4. They still visit each other regularly. _____

5. He is still in love with her. _____

6. They are still living in Quito. _____

7. We still see them at the club on Saturday night. _____

8. It is still raining. _____

DIRECT AND INDIRECT SPEECH

A direct quotation gives the words of a speaker exactly as spoken.

> **Tammy said, "I am leaving tomorrow."**

An indirect quotation reports on someone's words indirectly. The pronouns used in an indirect quotation are different from those in a direct quotation. (Review page 103 for sequence of tenses using *to say.*)

> **Tammy said that she was leaving tomorrow.**

When an indirect object is used in a sentence being changed from direct to indirect speech, *say to* is often changed to *tell.*

> **Direct: Barbara *said* to Phyllis, "I have a cold."**
>
> **Indirect: Barbara *told* Phyllis that she had a cold.**

Practice

 A *Change the following sentences from direct to indirect speech.*

1. Carolyn said, "I will be here at noon." *Carolyn said she would be here at noon.*

2. David said, "The plane will probably get in late." _____

3. The boss said, "I have to finish this report by tonight." _____

4. The doctor said, "She'll get well quickly." _____

5. The teacher said, "Everyone has to write a three-page paper for tomorrow." _____

6. Richard said, "I saw that movie last week." _____

7. Janie said, "I've read that book." _____

8. Suzanne said to her boyfriend, "I can't go tonight." _____

9. William said to me, "I'll finish this tomorrow." _____

10. She said to him, "The lights aren't working." _____

11. I said to the waitress, "This bill is wrong." _____

12. The boy said, "I'm only eight years old." _____

13. Henry said, "I can meet them later." _____

14. Ms. Bremer said, "I don't do business that way." _____

B *Change the following sentences to indirect speech.*

1. She said, "I need a vacation." *She said she needed a vacation.*

2. The teacher said, "The students need more practice in speaking." _____

3. The students said to the teacher, "These exercises are difficult for us." _____

4. Meredith said, "I don't feel well." _____

5. The teacher said to me, "Nobody can do that work as well as you." _____

6. Roberto said, "I'll be back soon."_____

7. The teacher said to us, "I may be a few minutes late." _____

8. Virginia said, "I have already seen that movie." _____

9. Steven said, "I'll see you this evening."_____

10. James said to us, "The baby is sleeping." _____

11. The children said, "We don't want to go home yet." _____

12. Janet said to me, "I got your message last night." _____

INDIRECT SPEECH

Questions

Questions in indirect speech are expressed as statements.

> Direct: Peter asked, "Where *does* Tanya *live?*"
>
> Indirect: Peter asked where Tanya *lived*.

Questions in indirect speech which are not introduced by a question word require the introduction of *whether* or *if*.

> Peter asked, "Does Tanya live near here?"
>
> Peter asked *whether* Tanya lived near here.
>
> Peter asked *if* Tanya lived near here.

Practice

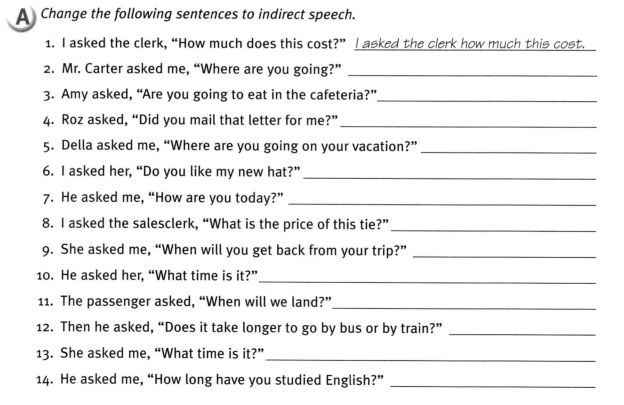

A *Change the following sentences to indirect speech.*

1. I asked the clerk, "How much does this cost?" *I asked the clerk how much this cost.*

2. Mr. Carter asked me, "Where are you going?" _____

3. Amy asked, "Are you going to eat in the cafeteria?" _____

4. Roz asked, "Did you mail that letter for me?" _____

5. Della asked me, "Where are you going on your vacation?" _____

6. I asked her, "Do you like my new hat?" _____

7. He asked me, "How are you today?" _____

8. I asked the salesclerk, "What is the price of this tie?" _____

9. She asked me, "When will you get back from your trip?" _____

10. He asked her, "What time is it?" _____

11. The passenger asked, "When will we land?" _____

12. Then he asked, "Does it take longer to go by bus or by train?" _____

13. She asked me, "What time is it?" _____

14. He asked me, "How long have you studied English?" _____

B *Choose the correct form.*

1. She asked me where (was I, I was) going. *She asked me where I was going.*

2. I don't know what (is his name, his name is). _____

3. Ask him what time (is it, it is). _____

4. The mail carrier wants to know where (she lives, does she live). _____

5. He asked me how much (did my car cost, my car cost). _____

6. I don't know where (did he put, he put) those magazines. _____

7. He wants to know where (do we have, we have) our English lesson. _____

8. I wonder what time (it is, is it). _____

9. Ask him how old (is he, he is). _____

10. He asked me how old (was I, I was). _____

11. Find out where (does she live, she lives). _____

12. I asked her where (she lived, did she live). _____

13. We asked her whether (was she, she was) married. _____

14. Nathan asked me how long (had I studied, I had studied) English. _____

15. He didn't say where (he was, was he) going. _____

16. Ask him where (is Helen, Helen is). _____

17. I forgot where (did I put, I put) it. _____

18. I don't know where (does he live, he lives). _____

19. He asked me when (I would, would I) return. _____

20. Brooke asked me where (was I, I was) going. _____

21. I asked him what time (could he, he could) meet us. _____

22. The supervisor asked me why (was I, I was) late for work. _____

C *Change each of the following questions to an indirect statement. Begin each one with the words given after it in parentheses.*

1. Where is the director's office? (I don't know *where the director's office is*.)

2. Where did Miss Dale go? (He wants to know _____.)

3. What time is it? (I wonder _____.)

Questions

4. Which file is the letter in? (Mr. Ames wants to know _____.)

5. How much does this cost? (I would like to know _____.)

6. How is he getting along? (The director wants to know _____.)

7. When is he leaving for the coast? (No one seems to know _____.)

8. When will Mr. Saki get back? (He asked me _____.)

9. What is the price of this book? (She said she didn't know _____.)

10. Where is he? (Do you know _____?)

11. Did he finish his test? (The teacher asked _____.)

12. Does he live in Berkeley? (Ask him _____.)

13. Where did you put it? (I forget _____.)

14. What does it mean? (I asked him _____.)

15. Where is she going? (I don't know _____.)

16. What time is he coming back? (He didn't tell me _____.)

17. Where is it? (I haven't any idea _____.)

18. Did she take it with her? (I really don't know _____.)

19. How well does she speak English? (He wants to know _____.)

20. Is he coming back today? (I'm not sure _____.)

21. Where is he going? (He didn't tell anyone _____.)

22. Did he return the book? (I don't know _____.)

Express orders or commands in indirect speech by using the infinitive form.

> He said to me, "Come back later."
>
> He told me *to come* back later.

> She said to me, "Don't wait for me."
>
> She told me not *to wait* for her.

Practice

 A *Change the following sentences from direct to indirect speech.*

1. My husband said to me, "Wait for me outside." <u>My husband told me to wait for him outside.</u>

2. The police officer said to us, "Don't make so much noise." _____

3. He told me, "Try to come on time." _____

4. He begged us, "Please send me some money at once." _____

5. He asked us, "Please sit down for a few minutes." _____

6. She said to me, "Don't forget what I have told you." _____

7. The teacher asked us, "Please be more careful when you write your reports."_____

8. He said to me angrily, "Don't make the same mistake again." _____

B *Change the following sentences to indirect speech.*

1. Wait outside in the hall. <u>The teacher told me to wait outside in the hall.</u>

2. Stay after class. _____

3. Don't make so much noise. _____

4. Look out the window, but don't open it. _____

5. Stop talking to Anna. _____

6. Sit up straight in your seat. _____

7. Be quiet while I am talking. _____

8. Pay more attention to what I say. _____

Past Form

Form the past tense of *should* and *ought to* with *have* and the past participle of the main verb.

> **You should study more.**
>
> **You *should have studied* more.**

> **He ought to finish his work.**
>
> **He *ought to have finished* his work.**

Note that the past tense forms of *should* and *ought to* have a negative force. They indicate that something was not done.

Practice

 A *Change the following sentences to past tense.*

1. He should study more before his exam. <u>*He should have studied more before his exam.*</u>

2. You should go to the beach with us. _____

3. She ought to prepare her work more carefully. _____

4. You should type your exercises. _____

5. You ought not to say such things to him. _____

6. We ought to call him. _____

7. You should visit Hawaii. _____

8. She ought to be put in the beginner's class. _____

9. The package should be sent air express. _____

10. You should speak to them in English. _____

11. They ought to buy a dog to protect the place. _____

12. He should tell her about it. _____

13. You should pay more attention to the grammar rules. _____

14. We should go to the beach instead of spending all day at home. _____

15. You ought to put some money in the bank each week. _____

16. You shouldn't be so generous with your money. _____

B *Using the past tense form of* should, *complete the following sentences in your own words.*

1. John went to the movies last night, but he *should have stayed at home and prepared his lessons* .

2. You waited for me on the corner of Juniper Street, but you _____.

3. He sent the letter by regular mail, but he _____.

4. Marsha came at eight o'clock, but she _____.

5. I went to the bus station to meet them, but I _____.

6. He gave Julie the money, but he _____.

7. She spoke to them in English, but she _____.

8. He took a business course in college, but he _____.

9. You prepared Lesson 10, but you _____.

10. I watched TV last night, but I _____.

11. Lucy put the letter on Ms. Doe's desk, but she _____.

12. We drove to New York, but we _____.

13. He went into business with his father, but he _____.

14. They spent their entire vacation in London, but they _____.

15. I called him at his office, but I _____.

16. He invested all his money in stocks, but he _____.

17. She gave the message to Mr. Sanders, but she _____.

18. He spent all his money on a new car, but he _____.

C *Repeat Exercise B using the past tense form of* ought to.

John went to the movies last night, but he *ought to have stayed at home and prepared his lessons* .

MUST HAVE, MAY HAVE

Must have (contracted as *must've*) indicates a strong probability that something happened in the past. It is followed by a past participle.

May have (no contracted form) indicates a possibility that something happened in the past. It is also followed by a past participle.

> Samantha *must've gone* home. (She probably went home.)
>
> Samantha *may have gone* home. (It is possible that she went home.)

Practice

A *Supply* must have *in the following sentences. Use both the full form and the contracted form. Use the past participle of the verb in parentheses.*

1. I can't find my book. I *must have left, must've left* (leave) it on the bus.

2. She _____ (take) the magazine with her. It's not here.

3. They don't answer their telephone. They _____ (go) away somewhere.

4. Roy _____ (study) hard before his examination.

5. She speaks English fluently. She _____ (study) a long time.

6. You _____ (see) her; she walked in front of you.

7. The bank _____ been _____ (rob) by professionals; they left no clues.

8. He _____ (come) by taxi.

B *Supply* may have *in the following sentences.*

1. She *may have taken* (take) the book by mistake.

2. They _____ (call) while you were out.

3. I _____ (leave) my keys at home or I _____ (lose) them somewhere. I'm not sure.

4. They _____ (be) wealthy at one time, but I doubt it.

5. They now think that the jewels _____ (steal) by one of the neighbors.

6. The storm _____ (delay) the plane.

C *Using* must have, *complete each of these sentences in your own words.*

1. They don't answer their phone; they *must have gone away on their vacation* .

2. I can't find my notebook; I _____.

3. William got very good grades this semester; he _____.

4. They seem to know a lot about Latin America; they _____.

5. He speaks English very well; he _____.

6. My umbrella has suddenly disappeared; Felix _____.

7. Daphne and Mark aren't playing volleyball anymore; they _____.

8. Sam didn't attend the meeting last night; he _____.

9. The streets are wet; it _____.

10. The plan worked perfectly; they _____.

D *Answer each of the following questions using* may have. *Add* I'm not sure *or* I don't know for sure *at the end of your answer.*

1. Did John bring his car to school today? *John may have brought his car to school today. I'm not sure.*

2. Did Professor Wiley learn Spanish in South America? _____

3. Did Helen call while I was out? _____

4. Was Mr. Reese born in Europe? _____

5. Did Mary and Helen have an argument? _____

6. Did he pass all his exams? _____

7. Did Grace go shopping this afternoon? _____

8. Were they married in Seattle? _____

9. Did it rain during the night? _____

10. Did the New York Yankees win the World Series last year? _____

CONDITIONAL SENTENCES

Future Possible

A conditional sentence has two clauses, a dependent clause beginning with *if* and a main clause.

> **If you study, you will pass your exam.**

In a future possible conditional sentence, the dependent clause is in the present tense and the main clause is in the future tense.

> **If I *have* enough money, I *will fly* to California.**

Practice

Supply the correct form of the verb in parentheses in order to make future possible conditions. Use contracted forms wherever possible.

1. If Melissa studies hard, she *'ll pass* (pass) her finals.

2. If I finish my work in time, I _____ (go) to the concert.

3. If I see Henry, I _____ (give) him your message.

4. If he works hard, he _____ (get) the raise.

5. If you don't hurry, we _____ (be) late for the meeting.

6. If he tries hard, he _____ (find) a job somewhere.

7. If he fails the test, he _____ (have) to repeat the course.

8. If the weather is nice tomorrow, we _____ (go) to the beach.

9. If Naomi arrives on time, I _____ (talk) to her.

10. If I have time tomorrow, I _____ (go) shopping with you.

11. If I _____ (find) the book, I will give it to you.

12. If the weather _____ (be) warm, we will go to the park tomorrow.

13. If you _____ (turn) out the light, we will be in the dark.

14. If you _____ (save) your money, you will be able to go on a vacation.

15. If you _____ (drive) slowly, you won't have any accidents.

16. If Jack _____ (call), I will speak with him.

17. If Susan _____ (learn) how to swim, she can go with us to the beach on Sundays.

Present Unreal

In a present unreal conditional sentence, the dependent clause is in the past tense and the main clause uses *would, should, could,* or *might.* The contracted forms *'d* and *n't* are often used.

> If you *studied,* you *would pass* your exam.
>
> If you *studied,* you'd *pass* your exam.

> If I *knew* better, I *wouldn't make* these mistakes.

Practice

Supply the form of the verb in parentheses in order to form present unreal conditions. Use the full form and the contracted form.

1. If I knew her well, I _would speak, 'd speak_ (speak) to her.

2. If he attended class regularly, he _____ (make) good progress.

3. If we had the money, we _____ (take) a trip to South America.

4. If he went to bed earlier, he _____ not (feel) so tired.

5. If he drove more carefully, he _____ (have) fewer accidents.

6. If John paid his debts, we _____ (respect) him more.

7. If I knew English better, I _____ (read) some English novels.

8. If he prepared his homework every night, he _____ (get) better grades.

9. If I _____ (own) an automobile, I would take a trip to California.

10. If she _____ (work) harder, she would probably get a better salary.

11. If I _____ (know) how to drive, I would buy a car.

12. If Louis knew more grammar, he _____ (make) fewer mistakes.

13. If he _____ not (waste) so much time in class, he would make better progress.

Dependent Clauses

Dependent clauses of present unreal conditional sentences use the past tense forms of all verbs except *to be*. *To be* uses *were* in all persons in these clauses.

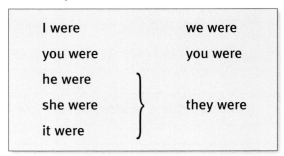

I were	we were
you were	you were
he were	
she were	they were
it were	

If I *were* you, I would study.

If he *were* here, he would answer your question.

Practice

A) *Supply the form of the verb in parentheses to make present unreal conditions.*

1. If I _____*were*_____ (be) you, I wouldn't mention it to her.

2. If today _____ (be) Saturday, I would not have to work.

3. If I _____ (be) in your position, I would think twice before doing that.

4. If today _____ (be) a holiday, we could go to the beach.

5. If the weather _____ (be) not so hot, I am sure she would feel better.

6. If Pete _____ (be) here, he would help us with this work.

7. If you _____ (be) a millionaire, how would you spend your time?

8. If George were here with us, I _____ (feel) more comfortable.

9. If they were really poor, they _____ not (be) able to live as they do.

10. If I were in Paris now, I _____ (go) to some of the summer concerts.

11. If Jill were here, she _____ (know) what to do.

12. If I were you, I _____ (tell) everyone the truth about the matter.

13. If I were a millionaire, I _____ (live) on the French Riviera.

14. If he were more ambitious, he _____ (try) to find a better job.

B *Complete the following sentences in your own words.*

1. I don't have a car, but if I *had one I would drive to California on my vacation* .

2. I am not in Florida now, but if I _____.

3. I don't like to swim, but if I _____.

4. I don't have enough money to buy a new car, but if I _____.

5. I can't type well, but if I _____.

6. I am not in your position, but if I _____.

7. I don't speak English perfectly, but if I _____.

8. I don't know how to play the piano, but if I _____.

9. Randy doesn't have much free time, but if he _____.

10. He never does his homework, but if he _____.

11. I am not a millionaire, but if I _____.

12. Today isn't a holiday, but if it _____.

C *In your own words, what would you do or what would happen . . .*

1. if you never did your homework? *If I never did my homework, I would fail all my tests.*

2. if you came to class late everyday? _____

3. if you found a large sum of money on the street? _____

4. if you lost your purse or wallet? _____

5. if you were ten years younger than you are? _____

6. if you failed all your exams? _____

7. if you knew English perfectly? _____

8. if you had a lot of free time? _____

Past Unreal

In a past unreal conditional sentence, the dependent clause is in the past perfect tense and the main clause uses *would have, should have, could have,* or *might have*. The contracted forms *'d have* and *'ve* are often used.

> If you *had studied,* you *would have passed* your exams.
>
> If you *had studied,* you*'d have passed* your exams.
>
> If you *had studied,* you *would've passed* your exams.

> If I *had known,* I *wouldn't have made* that mistake.

Practice

A *Supply the correct form of the verb in parentheses in order to make past unreal conditions. Use full forms and contracted forms.*

1. If I had known her, I <u>would have spoken, 'd have spoken, would've spoken</u> (speak) to her.

2. If he had learned the truth, he _____ (be) very angry.

3. If I had known that you needed me, I _____ (come) at once.

4. If they had invited us, naturally we _____ (go) to the party.

5. If you had worn your overcoat, you _____ not _____ (catch) cold.

6. If I had had your address, I _____ (write) to you.

7. If yesterday had been a holiday, I _____ (go) to the beach.

8. If you had asked me, I _____ (help) you.

9. If I _____ (know) about this yesterday, I would have worried all day long.

10. If the weather _____ (be) nice yesterday, we would have gone to the beach.

11. I would have looked you up if I _____ (know) you were living in Kansas.

12. I wouldn't have gotten wet if I _____ (wear) a raincoat.

13. If he _____ (study) more, he would have gotten better grades.

B *Complete the following sentences in your own words.*

1. She didn't make reservations, but if she <u>had made them, we all could have attended the grand opening</u>.

2. I didn't know your name, but if I _____.

3. Joan didn't have a car last winter, but if she _____.

4. We didn't have their phone number, but if we _____.

5. Lucille didn't get her car tuned up, but if she _____.

6. I didn't have enough money to take a vacation last summer, but if I _____.

7. I wasn't aware of the problem, but if I _____.

8. I didn't know how to speak English at that time, but if I _____.

9. He didn't study English before he came here, but if he _____.

10. He didn't come to class on time, but if he _____.

11. He didn't wear his overcoat, but if he _____.

12. There was no doctor present at the time of the accident, but if there _____.

C *In your own words, what would you have done or what would have happened . . .*

1. if you had come to class late? <u>The teacher would have been angry if I had come to class late.</u>

2. if yesterday had been a holiday? _____

3. if you had failed all your tests last semester? _____

4. if you had overslept this morning? _____

5. if yesterday had been your birthday? _____

6. if it had been raining when you left home this morning? _____

7. if yesterday had been Sunday? _____

8. if you had missed the bus this morning? _____

After *If, When, Until,* etc.

When dependent clauses introduced by *if* describe a future possible condition (review page 158), they use the present tense. Similarly, when dependent clauses introduced by *as long as, as soon as, before, unless, until, when,* and *while* describe a future condition, they also use the present tense.

> *If* it *rains,* we'll go inside.
>
> *When* it *rains,* we will go inside.
>
> *As soon as* it *rains,* we'll go inside.

> *If* the telephone *rings* while I'm out, please answer it.

Practice

Supply the proper form of the verbs in parentheses.

1. We will stay outside until it ___rains___ (rain).

2. If the weather _____ (be) nice next Sunday, we will go to the mountains.

3. If the workers _____ (go) on strike, production will be greatly reduced.

4. Please watch my bag while I _____ (get) my ticket.

5. Please call me as soon as you _____ (get) back from your trip.

6. I won't go unless they _____ (invite) me.

7. If the river _____ (rise) much higher, there will be a flood.

8. Don't leave until I _____ (call) you.

9. If it _____ (rain) next Saturday, I may have to cancel my trip.

10. When the weather _____ (get) warmer, we can go swimming.

11. I plan to wait here until the mail _____ (arrive).

12. If you _____ not _____ (arrive) on time, you will not get a seat.

13. When you _____ (see) the light turn red, be sure to stop your car.

14. If you _____ (sit) in the sun too long, you may get burned.

15. Give him this memorandum as soon as you _____ (see) him.

Wish usually suggests a situation that is unreal or contrary to fact. After *wish*—as in unreal conditional statements—use a past tense clause to suggest present action and a past perfect tense clause to suggest past action.

Present:	I *wish* she *were* here now.
Past:	I *wish* I had *known* about this yesterday.

The expressions *I wish you would* and *I wish you wouldn't* are used to express polite commands or requests.

I wish you would stay here.	**I wish you wouldn't go home.**

Practice

 A *Supply the correct form of the verbs in parentheses.*

1. I wish I __owned__ (own) a video recorder.
2. Ed wishes he _____ (be) a mechanical engineer.
3. I wish I _____ (go) to the movie with you last night.
4. I wish I _____ (have) today off so I could go swimming.
5. I wish I _____ (have) yesterday off so I could have gone swimming.
6. I wish I _____ (be) in Florida now.
7. I wish you _____ (live) near me.
8. I wish that, for just a day, I _____ (be) President of the United States.
9. I wish I _____ (can) help you, but I can't.
10. I wish I _____ (study) harder when I was young.

B *Begin these imperative sentences with* I wish you would *or* I wish you wouldn't, *making them more polite.*

1. Come back in an hour. *I wish you would come back in an hour.*
2. Mail this letter right away, Kevin. _____
3. Be creative in your writing. _____
4. Don't make any mistakes. _____
5. Help me with this problem. _____

In order to avoid repetition of earlier words or phrases, use *too* or *so* and an appropriate auxiliary verb in affirmative sentences.

> **He speaks English and she speaks English.**
>
> **He speaks English and she *does too*.**
>
> **He speaks English and *so does* she.**

> **I went to New York and Jay went to New York.**
>
> **I went to New York and Jay *did too*.**
>
> **I went to New York and *so did* Jay.**

Practice

 A *Shorten the following sentences by using a verb phrase with* too.

1. He wants to go there, and she wants to go there. <u>He wants to go there, and she does too.</u>

2. Liz left right after lunch, and Bob left right after lunch. _____

3. She is going to the concert, and I am going to the concert. _____

4. Kay will be here at ten o'clock, and I will be here at ten o'clock. _____

5. My watch is fast, and your watch is fast. _____

6. She wanted to go to a movie, and I wanted to go to a movie. _____

7. She is making good progress, and her brother is making good progress. _____

8. Evan has gone back to Europe, and his wife has gone back to Europe. _____

9. Bert was arrested, and his assistant was arrested. _____

10. He saw the accident, and I saw the accident. _____

11. Beth liked the movie, and I liked the movie. _____

12. Nan will be there, and her sister will be there. _____

13. We go to the beach every weekend, and they go to the beach every weekend. _____

14. Mark can speak French, and she can speak French. _____

15. I have had lunch, and Cy has had lunch. _____

B *Shorten the sentences in Exercise A by using a verb phrase with* so.

He wants to go there, and she wants to go there. *He wants to go there, and so does she.*

EITHER, NEITHER

Use *either* and *neither* to avoid repetition in negative sentences.

> He doesn't bowl, and she doesn't bowl.
>
> He doesn't bowl, and she doesn't *either*.
>
> He doesn't bowl, and *neither* does she.

> I didn't go to Boston, and Hal didn't go to Boston.
>
> I didn't go to Boston, and Hal didn't *either*.
>
> I didn't go to Boston, and *neither* did Hal.

Practice

A *Shorten the following sentences (avoiding repetition) by using a verb phrase with* either.

1. He doesn't want to go, and she doesn't want to go. *He doesn't want to go, and she doesn't either.*

2. Grace didn't like the movie, and I didn't like the movie. _____

3. She won't be here, and her sister won't be here. _____

4. She hasn't ever been in China, and I haven't ever been in China. _____

5. Lew hadn't seen the movie, and I hadn't seen the movie. _____

6. He would never say such a thing, and I would never say such a thing. _____

7. Margaret can't swim, and I can't swim. _____

8. He doesn't know her well, and I don't know her well. _____

9. Your watch isn't right, and mine isn't right. _____

10. I don't like to dance, and my wife doesn't like to dance. _____

11. Mr. Rogers wasn't at the meeting, and Mr. Barker wasn't at the meeting. _____

12. I couldn't hear the speaker, and my friend couldn't hear the speaker. _____

13. You won't enjoy that movie, and your son won't enjoy that movie. _____

14. We don't have a television set, and they don't have a television set. _____

B *Shorten the sentences in Exercise A by using a verb phrase with* neither.

He doesn't want to go, and she doesn't want to go. *He doesn't want to go, and neither does she.*

In sentences describing two opposite situations, avoid repetition with *but* and an appropriate auxiliary.

> **She liked the movie. I didn't like the movie.**
>
> **She liked the movie,** *but* I *didn't*.

> **He can't speak English. His wife speaks English.**
>
> **He can't speak English,** *but* his wife *can*.

Practice

 A *Complete the following sentences by adding the necessary auxiliary verb.*

1. She dances well, but her sister _doesn't_ .

2. I know how to swim, but Francis _____.

3. She can speak French, but her husband _____.

4. I'll be there, but Jimmy _____.

5. They didn't like the movie, but we _____.

6. Alex agrees with you, but I _____.

7. George used to be the best student in the class, but now Ralph _____.

8. At first I didn't like the new manager, but now I _____.

9. Henry won't be able to attend the meeting, but Alice _____.

10. I have never been in Australia, but my wife _____.

11. Ben has seen the movie, but I _____.

12. He enjoys living in Florida, but his wife _____.

13. She knows how to swim, but her friend _____.

14. She is a serious student, but her sister _____.

15. My husband likes golf, but I _____.

16. They are going to the beach, but I _____.

17. They don't have classes tomorrow, but we _____.

18. He knows her, but I _____.

19. Gail likes to study mathematics, but I _____.

20. She is good at mathematics, but I _____.

B *Complete the following sentences with the necessary auxiliaries.*

1. Eunice isn't going to the party, but I ___*am*___.

2. Michael will be there, but Michele _____.

3. Alexandra will go, and so _____ her husband.

4. Winnie speaks Chinese, and so _____ Penny.

5. Patrick isn't going to the party, and neither _____ his brother.

6. You say you're not going to the party, but I'm sure you _____.

7. Sandy has gone away for the summer, and so _____ Kevin.

8. Polly went to the movies last night, and Carson _____, too.

9. She isn't a good driver, and he _____ either.

10. He can't go, but I _____.

11. I can't swim, and she _____ either.

12. She says she knows him well, but I don't think she _____.

13. I knew Scotty wouldn't come, but I thought Karen _____.

14. At first they thought they couldn't go, but now they think they _____.

15. She won't drive at night, but I _____.

16. At first I didn't like living in the United States, but now I _____.

17. I haven't seen that play, but my daughters _____.

18. Professor Schultz can't speak German and neither _____ her husband.

19. Mr. Schultz can speak Russian, but his wife _____.

20. My parents like living in California, but I _____.

21. Cindy doesn't want to go, and neither _____ I.

Negative questions are usually formed by placing a contracted form of *to be* or an auxiliary verb and *not* before the subject. When a question word is used, it is placed before the contraction.

She is here today.	*Isn't* she here today?
Peter saw them.	*Didn't* Peter see them?
Why isn't she here today?	*Why didn't* Peter see them?

Practice

A *Change the following sentences to negative questions. Use only contracted forms.*

1. Maurice didn't attend the meeting. *Didn't Maurice attend the meeting?*

2. Conrad isn't changing the oil in his car now. _____

3. Helene won't be here today. _____

4. She won't be here tomorrow either. _____

5. Andrea didn't take the accounting test yesterday. _____

6. Colleen doesn't like to study in the morning. _____

7. We don't like to get up early. _____

8. They aren't going with us to the movie tonight. _____

9. Mr. Donahue didn't bring the food. _____

10. It isn't raining. _____

11. It wasn't raining this morning either. _____

12. It hasn't rained all week. _____

13. The Starskys aren't moving to Cleveland. _____

B *Change the sentences in Exercise A to questions beginning with* Why.

Maurice didn't attend the meeting. *Why didn't Maurice attend the meeting?*

Form subject questions by substituting *who*, *what*, or *which* for the subject of a sentence or for the modifiers of the subject.

Stephanie lives here.	*Who* lives here?
The vase is on the table.	*What* is on the table?
The blue ribbon is his.	*Which* ribbon is his?

Practice

Change the following sentences to questions beginning with the question words in parentheses.

1. Grace broke the dish. (Who) *Who broke the dish?*_____

2. February comes before March. (Which month) _____

3. Coffee is one of the chief exports of Brazil. (What)_____

4. Lee drove the car. (Who) _____

5. His carelessness caused the accident (What) _____

6. The red umbrella belongs to her. (Which umbrella) _____

7. The black notebook is hers. (Which notebook)_____

8. The Number 5 bus goes to the airport. (Which bus) _____

9. The Reillys live next door to them. (Who) _____

10. Mexico is south of the United States. (Which country)_____

11. She is the best student in the class. (Who) _____

12. Decreased demand causes a fall in prices. (What) _____

13. Bob has your book. (Who)_____

14. The Atlantic Ocean is east of the United States. (What ocean) _____

15. George won first prize in the contest. (Who) _____

16. This book is mine. (Which) _____

17. That woman is my mother. (Who)_____

18. Bernard is doing his homework now. (Who) _____

An appropriate form of *to have* or *to get* plus the past participle is used to show that the subject caused someone else to perform an action.

I often *have* my shoes *shined*.	I often *get* my shoes *shined*.
He *had* the work *done* by an expert.	He *got* the work *done* by an expert.
Did she *have* her house *painted?*	*Did* she *get* her house *painted?*

Practice

 A *Change these sentences to the causative form first with* have *and then with* get.

1. I cut my hair once a month. *I have my hair cut once a month. I get my hair cut once a month.*

2. We'll change the oil in our car soon. _____

3. I should clean and wax the kitchen floor. _____

4. You typed those letters yesterday. _____

5. They checked the oxygen level in their fish tank. _____

6. Phil is going to dry clean his winter coat. _____

7. Did she repair her computer? _____

8. I should repair the hole in my shoes. _____

B *Add a past participle plus your own words to form causative form sentences.*

1. We should have our house *repainted this summer* _____.

2. I'm going to get this watch _____.

3. She had her suit _____.

4. They had their portrait _____.

5. You always get your rugs _____.

6. I wanted to have the wedding _____.

7. The twins go to Claude's to get their hair _____.

8. He always gets his teeth _____.

EXCLAMATIONS

To emphasize a noun, use *what* or *what a* and an exclamation point *(!)*.

***What* beauty!**	***What a* beautiful painting!**

To emphasize an adjective or adverb in a sentence, use *how* and an exclamation point.

***How* fantastic!**	***How* well she swims!**	***How* tall he is!**

Practice

Change these sentences to exclamations which emphasize some part of them. Use what, what a, *or* how *and an exclamation point.*

1. David reads fast. *How fast David reads!* _____

2. It's a beautiful day. _____

3. He is a good-looking boy. _____

4. Gail plays golf well. _____

5. They speak English fluently. _____

6. Pauline is tall. _____

7. It is hot today. _____

8. It is a hot day. _____

9. You have good taste in clothes. _____

10. That's a gorgeous car. _____

11. She is a lucky card player. _____

12. We're having beautiful weather now. _____

13. Penny looks very old. _____

14. It was an interesting movie. _____

15. The lake is very wide. _____

16. That was very strange behavior. _____

Show emphasis in affirmative statements by adding *do, does,* or *did* to show strong feeling. Use the simple form of the verb.

> She knows him.   She *does* know him.
>
> I called you.   I *did* call you.

Show emphasis in imperative statements by adding *do.*

> Sit down.   *Do* sit down.

Practice

Make these sentences more emphatic by changing the italicized verb.

1. She *lives* on a houseboat. I'm sure of it. *She does live on a houseboat. I'm sure of it.*

2. I *wrote* that letter. I am positive of it. _____

3. Ed *took* the book. He told me so. _____

4. But we *studied* that exercise. _____

5. You're mistaken. I *want* to learn English. _____

6. I *did* it yesterday. _____

7. *Call* me again sometime. _____

8. I maintain that she *lives* in West Virginia. _____

9. Sam didn't visit me, but he *called* me on the phone. _____

10. Columbus didn't reach the Indies, but he *reached* a new continent._____

11. Maps were very poor then, but they *showed* that the earth was round._____

12. Rick doesn't study hard, but he *attends* class regularly. _____

13. I didn't go away on my vacation, but I *had* a good rest._____

14. *Bring* Sue with you the next time you come._____

15. *Visit* us again sometime. _____

16. She really *seems* to enjoy her new guitar. _____

Informal Usage

In everyday conversation, avoid beginning a question with a preposition. Put the preposition at the end of the sentence.

> **What are they looking *at?***
>
> **What country does he come *from?***

Practice

Supply the necessary prepositions at the end of these sentences.

1. What are they talking ____*about*____?
2. What are you thinking _____?
3. What country was he born _____?
4. Whom (who) do you wish to speak _____?
5. What kind of car are you looking _____?
6. Whom (who) does this book belong _____?
7. What are they going to use the money _____?
8. Which restaurant do you want to eat _____?
9. Which shop did she buy the dress _____?
10. Whom (who) was the book written _____?
11. Which hotel did he go _____?
12. Whom (who) did they sell their house _____?
13. Which magazine do you want to look _____?
14. What is the guide pointing _____?
15. Which room do you have your lesson _____?
16. Where did all that dirt come _____?
17. What are you smiling _____?

Informal Usage

Informal usage permits moving a preposition with a relative pronoun object to the end of the sentence.

> **This is the textbook *which* I was talking *about*.**
>
> **Janice was the accountant *whom* you spoke *to*.**

In sentences with this construction, the relative pronoun may be dropped altogether.

> **This is the textbook I was talking *about*.**
>
> **Janice was the accountant you spoke *to*.**

Practice

 A *Change the preposition's position from before the relative pronoun to the end of the sentence or clause.*

1. This is the book about which everyone is talking. *This is the book which everyone is talking about.*

2. The man *to whom* you were speaking is Dr. Evans. _____

3. This is the room *in which* they found the clue. _____

4. He is the kind of salesman *from whom* it is difficult to get away. _____

5. The person *to whom* you should speak is Miss Williams. _____

6. It is a subject *on which* we will never agree. _____

7. The thing *about which* they were arguing was really of little importance. _____

8. It is a place *in which* you feel at home. _____

9. It was Bob *for whom* we had to wait so long. _____

10. It was Liz *from whom* he borrowed the money. _____

11. The room *in which* we study is on the second floor. _____

12. This is the street *on which* they live. _____

13. I finally found the book *for which* I was looking. _____

14. The students *with whom* she studies are mainly from South America. _____

15. The fellow *with whom* I roomed was from Chicago. _____

B *Change the position of the preposition and drop the relative pronoun in the sentences in Exercise A.*

This is the book *about which* everyone is talking. *This is the book everyone is talking about.*

Comma

Commas separate words, phrases, or clauses in a series.

> We need books, pencils, and chairs.
>
> We played tennis, took walks, and went swimming.

Commas set off days of the week, dates, addresses, and geographical names.

> He lives in Chicago, Illinois.
>
> It happened on Friday, October 9, 1998.

Commas set off parenthetical expressions, words in direct address, and appositives.

> He was, to be sure, an excellent diplomat.
>
> And so, my friends, you can see the results.
>
> Mr. Santini, our neighbor, was hurt recently.

Practice

Punctuate the following sentences.

1. We study history mathematics geography and reading. *We study history, mathematics, geography, and reading.*

2. Roberta the mechanic repaired our car and also fixed our refrigerator. _____

3. We cannot of course reveal our sources. _____

4. Johnnie Reese the president of our class spent the night at our house. _____

5. He did not in the first place tell the whole story. _____

6. She was born in Scranton Pennsylvania on March 23 1973 and she has lived there ever since. _____

7. We cannot after all live forever. _____

8. By the way do you remember Zan's address? _____

9. Marlene Henry's cousin is visiting him at his home in Madison Wisconsin. _____

10. Where were you Mr. Jones on the morning of February 12 2001? _____

11. The old Amos Building a famous landmark of the town was recently torn down. _____

    As a matter of fact it was torn down on February 12 Lincoln's birthday. _____

12. The most popular summer sports are tennis swimming and hiking._____

13. Yesterday I met quite by accident two former schoolmates Palmer and Stewart. _____

14. I last saw them on graduation day June 20 1998. _____

Comma and Semicolon

Nonrestrictive clauses do not limit or define; they are parenthetic and are set off by commas.

> **Dick, who is clever, passes all his exams.**
>
> **San Francisco, where we met, is a beautiful city.**

Restrictive clauses identify or define the antecedent noun. They are not parenthetical and are not set off by commas.

> **Any boy who is clever passes all his exams.**
>
> **The place where we met is a beautiful city.**

Practice

Punctuate the following sentences.

1. Amy who is lazy does not deserve to pass. _Amy, who is lazy, does not deserve to pass._

2. Any student who is lazy does not deserve to pass. _____

3. Any girl who has brown hair will be all right for the part of the heroine. _____

4. Mary who has brown hair was selected for the part of the heroine. _____

5. Little Teddy's hands which were covered with tar were very hard to clean. _____

6. Any passenger who enters the engine room does so at his or her own risk. _____

7. The man who said that is a liar. _____

8. Mr. Pace who told the story was obviously lying. _____

9. Wednesday when my brother is usually out of town will be a good day to call. _____

10. Mr. Hemmingway who was bored with the real estate business decided to move to Glen Acres which was formerly a swamp. _____

11. The man who was laughing was probably the one who played the practical joke. _____

12. Her hair which she painstakingly combed every morning was very neat._____

13. The profit which you can expect on so cheap an article is very small. _____

14. We heard a noise that resembled the cry of an injured animal._____

15. The George Washington Bridge which spans the Hudson River has been repaired recently. _____

Comma and Semicolon

Use a comma before a conjunction joining two independent clauses.

> **In the North there are many wheat fields, but cotton fields predominate in the South.**
>
> **We had trouble reaching him, but at last he answered.**

If two independent clauses are closely related in meaning, but are not connected by a conjunction, join them with a semicolon.

> **In the North there are many wheat fields; in the South cotton fields predominate.**
>
> **We had trouble reaching him; at last, however, he answered.**

Practice

 Punctuate the following sentences.

1. Chicago is my favorite city but Philadelphia has more diversity. *Chicago is my favorite city, but Philadelphia has more diversity.*

2. The general manager will talk to you soon and will give you the information. _____

3. Smith is a very good automobile mechanic and his prices are low. _____

4. She kept the money for more than a month and then finally returned it. _____

5. She kept the book for a long time but she finally returned it. _____

6. She kept the letters for a long time then she finally returned them. _____

7. There were six ambassadors and their entrance was a gaudy spectacle. _____

8. Andy didn't go but his wife did. _____

9. Maxine was pleased with the results but her husband wasn't. _____

10. Gloria and Edith were cautious but Archie bet on the small horse and won more than a hundred dollars. _____

11. Betty plays the piano and Ginger plays the violin. _____

12. Frank plays the saxophone Alexis plays the cornet. _____

13. His clothes were filthy but everyone knew that he was still the boss. _____

14. I got to the meeting on time but no one was there. _____

15. It's cold in the winter it's hot in the summer. _____

Comma and Semicolon

B *Punctuate the following sentences.*

1. The changes which we are planning will soon be completed then we will be able to serve you. *The changes which we are planning will soon be completed; then we will be able to serve you.*

2. Jenny and Miss Smith came into the room looked around whispered to each other and then strangely enough walked out. _____

3. William's store which sells many fancy groceries was recently repainted as a consequence it now looks very nice indeed. _____

4. I am sure that Mary will like our new house which was built by that famous architect Mr. James. _____

5. We drove from Harrisburg Pennsylvania to Albany which is the capital of New York State.

   _____

6. Joan and Ellen stopped and watched Henry and Joseph running and jumping.

   _____

7. We Ida Ethel and I considered going but later we changed our collective minds and decided to stay at home and rest. _____

8. The man whom I saw yesterday was Ben Reese's brother Tim Reese who is an eye specialist. _____

9. Saturday January 16 2003 was the coldest day that we had however the next day Sunday seemed even colder to me but of course I am very sensitive to cold. _____

   _____

10. Everyone climbed into the wagon then we started out and soon we were far out in the country it was lovely. _____

11. At eleven John adjourned the meeting no decision having been reached by that time.

    _____

12. I believe that Mr. Davis should be notified at once yet we all realize that the duty is not a pleasant one. _____

13. Cities that don't have good public transportation systems are considered impossible to live in by Dr. Reynolds who doesn't own a car. _____

14. Commas I noted are useful punctuation marks. _____

15. Come here at once I need you immediately! _____

16. Did you see her yesterday are you going to see her tomorrow? _____

17. When will we finish this exercise Robert? _____

Advice/Advise

Advice is a noun, *advise* is a verb.

> The counselor *advised* me to take a writing course; I'll follow her *advice.*

As far as/Until

As far as refers to distance; *until* refers to time.

> She walked *as far as* the corner and then turned back.
>
> She said she could stay only *until* ten o'clock.

Beat/Win

One *beats* teams or opponents; one *wins* games.

> Tracey *won* the tennis match by *beating* Sandra in three sets.

Do/Make

The differences between these verbs are idiomatic. Both have the meaning *to accomplish* or *to perform.* Note these uses:

> This morning I *made* the bed and then *made* breakfast. Afterwards I *did* the dishes. I always *do* the housework before I *do* my exercises.
>
> I *made* a phone call, but I *made* a mistake when I dialed.

In/Into

In suggests position within a certain space; *into* suggests action toward a certain point.

> I made sure there was water *in* the pool before I dived *into* it.

Rob/Steal

One *steals* an object; one *robs* a person or thing.

> They *robbed* the bank and then *stole* a car to get away.

Pour/Spill

Spill suggests an accidental or unintentional action; *pour* suggests an intentional one.

> As I *was pouring* my tea into my cup, I *spilled* some on the floor.

Practice

Choose the word in parentheses which correctly completes each sentence.

1. We rode the bus (as far as, until) the waterfront. _We rode the bus as far as the waterfront._

2. I hope I don't (do, make) a mistake on my final exam. _____

3. What do you (advice, advise) me to do? _____

4. Unknowingly, she walked right (in, into) their trap. _____

5. My sister usually (beats, wins) me when we play Ping-Pong. _____

6. James tripped and (poured, spilled) his soup. _____

7. Yesterday someone (robbed, stole) my briefcase. _____

8. This class lasts (as far as, until) 9:30. _____

9. Stephanie is always ready to give us her (advice, advise). _____

10. The bartender carefully (poured, spilled) the martini from the pitcher. _____

11. Did the thieves (rob, steal) your parents' home again? _____

12. The money was already (in, into) the drawer. _____

13. Did you (do, make) lasagna for dinner last night? _____

14. Who (does, makes) the dishes in your house, you or your brother? _____

15. I don't usually (beat, win) when I play chess, but I'm learning. _____

16. I (advice, advise) you to (pour, spill) some of the milk out of that bowl in order to avoid (pouring, spilling) it. _____

17. Who (robbed, stole) the calculator I left (in, into) my desk? _____

18. He rode with me (as far as, until) Lake Ontario. _____

Beside/Besides

Beside means *next to*; *besides* means *in addition to*.

> ***Besides*** me, three others went on the trip. I sat ***beside*** Bart on the bus.

Few/Less

Few is used only with plural countable nouns; *less* is used only with noncountable nouns.

> | | |
> |---|---|
> | *few* books | *less* time |
> | *few* pencils | *less* sugar |

Few/A few; Little/A little

Few and *little* have a negative force and suggest the absence of some quantity or thing; *a few* and *a little* have a positive force and suggest the presence of a quantity or thing, although in small amount.

> He has many enemies and *few* friends.
>
> He is not completely alone. He still has *a few* friends.

Forget/Leave

One can *leave* something in a particular place, but one *cannot forget* something in a particular place.

> I *have forgotten* my book. I *left* it at home.
>
> (Not: I have forgotten my book at home.)

No/Not

No is an adjective used to modify nouns. *Not* is an adverb used to modify verbs and before *much, many, any, enough,* and any article or numeral modifying a noun.

> She has *no* money and does *not* speak their language.
>
> *Not* many people came; there were probably *not* even 50 there.

Too/Very

Very means *much* or *to a large degree*. *Too* always suggests something in excess, more of something than we need or can use. *Too* is often followed by an infinitive construction.

> This book is *very* big, but it will fit in my pocket.
>
> This book is *too* big *to fit* in my pocket.

Used to/To be used to (See also page 123.)

Used to describes a habitual past action which is no longer in force. *To be used to* means *to be accustomed to.* Notice that *to be used to* is followed by a noun construction because the *to* in this case is not the sign of an infinitive but a preposition.

> John *used to* study with Miss Smith.
>
> John *is used to* studying with Miss Smith and therefore doesn't wish to change teachers.

Practice

Choose the word in parentheses which correctly completes each sentence.

1. Victor spends (few, little) time on his English. _Victor spends little time on his English._

2. I (am used to, used) riding on the subway; I don't mind it. _____

3. This soup is (too, very) hot to eat. _____

4. This is a (too, very) heavy chair, but I think I can move it. _____

5. Now that we have five children, we have (few, less) room than before. _____

6. Four girls (beside, besides) Sally left for camp on the bus. _____

7. Connie sits (beside, besides) me in my chemistry class. _____

8. I (left, forgot) my coat at school today. _____

9. There are (no, not) Spanish speakers in our class. _____

10. There are (no, not) many Spanish speakers in our class. _____

11. There is (no, not) enough support for our program; thus, we do (no, not) have the money to remain open. _____

12. Steve is so silly that he often (leaves, forgets) his own name. _____

Borrow/Lend

One *borrows* something from someone or something; one *lends* something to someone or something.

> *Lend* me your pen, please; I only want to *borrow* it for a minute.

Despite/In spite of

Despite and *in spite of* have the same meaning and can be used interchangeably. Note, however, that when a clause rather than a noun follows these prepositions, the construction *despite the fact* or *in spite of the fact* must be used.

> He came *despite* the rain.
>
> He came *despite the fact* that it was raining.
>
> He came *in spite of* the rain.
>
> He came *in spite of the fact* that it was raining.

Teach/Learn

Learn means to "gain knowledge"; *teach* means "to instruct someone else."

> I *learned* French last year; now I'll *teach* it to you.

Infinitives without *To*

Infinitives without *to* are used after the verbs *let, make, hear, see,* and *feel.*

> He *let* me *borrow* his bicycle.   She *made* us *wait* an hour.

Negative Openings

If a sentence begins with a negative word, an auxiliary verb (or some form of *to be*) must precede the subject, as in interrogative sentences.

> *Never have* I heard such music.
>
> *Not* once *did* he mention your name.

Singular and Plural Forms in Measurements

Use the singular form of such words as *foot, dollar, year,* etc., when such words are used as adjectives; use the plural form when such words are used alone as nouns.

> He signed a five-*year* contract.
>
> This contract runs for five *years*.

Practice

Choose the word in parentheses which correctly completes each sentence.

1. The painters are using a twenty (feet, foot) ladder to climb up that building. *The painters are using a twenty-foot ladder to climb up that building.*

2. I want to (borrow, lend) your car for an hour. Will you please (borrow, lend) it to me?

3. (Despite, Despite the fact) the heat, we decided not to go to the beach._____

4. I missed class yesterday so I wonder if you would (borrow, lend) me your notes. _____

5. Who (taught, learned) you how to ice-skate? _____

6. We went for a walk (despite, despite the fact) that the weather was bad._____

7. Never (I have seen, have I seen) Justin so angry. _____

8. Amanda is going to (teach, learn) me how to play tennis._____

9. What have you (learned, taught) from your teacher this year? _____

10. I saw the thief (to take, take) the money. _____

11. Not once (the speaker mentioned, did the speaker mention) the subject of foreign aid.

12. The doctor made us (wait, to wait) two hours in her office._____

13. Nowhere (you could find, could you find) a more generous person. _____

14. Kareem is a seven (feet, foot) tall basketball player. When he was fifteen years old he was already six (feet, foot) tall. _____

15. (In spite of, in spite of the fact) that he was ill, Gerald attended each session of the conference. _____

16. I haven't heard them (make, to make) a sound for hours. _____

17. I work in a thirty-four (story, stories) building. _____

18. My sister never has enough money; she is always (lending, borrowing) some from me until her next paycheck. _____

Parts of Speech

There are 8 parts of speech in English.

Part of Speech	Description	Examples
Noun	Nouns refer to people, places, or things.	The young **driver** turned her new **car** quickly into a busy **street**. Bang! She hit a huge yellow **bus** and came to a stop.
Adjective	Adjectives describe nouns.	The **young** driver turned her **new** car quickly into a **busy** street. Bang! She hit a **huge yellow** bus and came to a stop.
Verb	Verbs refer to an action or a state of being (*is*).	The young driver **turned** her new car quickly into a busy street. Bang! She **hit** a huge yellow bus and **came** to a stop.
Adverb	Adverbs describe verbs, adjectives, and other adverbs.	The young driver turned her new car **quickly** into a busy street. Bang! She hit a huge yellow bus and came to a stop.
Conjunction	Conjunctions join two parts of a sentence or phrase.	The young driver turned her new car quickly into a busy street. Bang! She hit a huge yellow bus **and** came to a stop.
Pronoun	Pronouns replace nouns.	The young driver turned **her** new car quickly into a busy street. Bang! **She** hit a huge yellow bus and came to a stop.
Preposition	Prepositions introduce phrases of time, place, or how something is done.	The young driver turner her new car quickly **into** a busy street. Bang! She hit a huge yellow bus and came to a stop.
Interjection	Interjections express strong emotions or sensations.	The young driver turned her new car quickly into a busy street. **Bang!** She hit a huge yellow bus and came to a stop.

Subject + Verb

A sentence can consist simply of a subject (a noun or pronoun) and a verb.

Subject	Verb
Fernando	arrived.
Alex	left.

Subject + Verb + Direct Object

A sentence can consist of a subject, a verb, and a direct object. A direct object answers the question, *what?* (*He had what? He had a letter. Julio wanted what? Julio wanted ice cream.*) Some verbs, like *have,* are always followed by a direct object.

Subject	Verb	Direct Object
Veronique	threw	the ball.
Evan	liked	Susan.
He	had	a suitcase.

Subject + Verb + Indirect Object

Sentences can also have indirect objects. An indirect object answers the question, *to whom?* (*He wrote to whom? He wrote to Junko. Junko gave the letter to whom? Junko gave Aoko the letter.*)

If the indirect object appears **after** the direct object, you must use *to.*

If the indirect object appears **after** the verb but **before** the direct object, you do not use *to.*

Subject	Verb	Direct Object	Indirect Object
He	gave	the suitcase	to his brother.

Subject	Verb	Indirect Object	Direct Object
He	gave	his brother	the suitcase.
He	gave	him	the suitcase.

Simple, Compound, and Complex Sentences

Simple Sentences

Simple sentences have only one clause. (A *clause* is a group of words with a subject and a verb.) But simple sentences can have more than one subject, verb, and direct object. These are called *compound* subjects, verbs, and direct objects.

One subject One verb	Compound Subjects	Compound Verbs	Compound Direct Objects
Chen is busy.	**He** and **his friends** go out on weekends.	He **goes** to school and also **works.**	He likes **music** and **movies.**

Compound Sentences

Compound sentences have **two** or more clauses joined by a **coordinating** conjunction. Some common coordinating conjunctions are *and, but,* and *or.* The two clauses of a compound sentence are always separated by a comma.

Clause 1		Clause 2
Chen works hard at school,	**and**	he gets good grades.
He studies during the week,	**but**	he has fun on weekends.
He and his friends see a movie,	**or**	they go to a concert.

Complex Sentences

Complex sentences have two clauses joined by a **subordinating** conjunction. Some common subordinating conjunctions are *when, because,* and *that.*

Clause 1		Clause 2
Chen feels tired	**when**	he gets home at night.
He is tired	**because**	he worked hard.
He wishes	**that**	he could go to a movie.

Common Nouns and Proper Nouns

Common nouns refer to any person, place, or thing.

People	Places	Things
child	library	television
police officer	city	baseball

Proper nouns refer to the names of specific people, places, and things. Proper nouns are always written with a capital letter.

People	Places	Things
Tiger Woods	Brazil	Microsoft Corporation
Shakira	Toronto	Academy Awards
Albert Einstein	Yankee Stadium	Philadelphia Orchestra

Count and Noncount Nouns

You can count some things: four apples, two trees, three houses. These are count nouns.

You can't count other things: some water, lots of grass, a handful of flour. These are noncount nouns.

Count nouns can be **singular** (just one) or **plural** (more than one).

I ate an **apple.**	She ate two **apples.**

Noncount nouns can only be singular.

(Some words, such as *information* and *advice* are noncount nouns in English, but they are count nouns in some other languages.)

Some, a little, lots are examples of words that can be used with noncount nouns to reflect quantities. Do not use *a* or *an* with noncount nouns.

Correct	Incorrect
some money	a money
lots of mail	one mail
a little advice	an advice

Articles

A and *an* can only mean *one.* Use *a* and *an* with count nouns when the noun is indefinite. Use *an* before a vowel sound and *a* before a consonant sound.

> I ate **an** apple and **a** banana. (It can be any apple or banana.)

The is an article that is used with specific count or noncount nouns. The listener knows specifically which person, place, or thing the speaker is talking about.

> I ate an apple. Then I ate a banana. **The** apple was better. (We know *which* apple the speaker is talking about. It is the apple she just ate.)
>
> I bought some water and some soda. **The** water was cold. (We know *which* water the speaker is talking about. It is the water he just bought.)

Forming Plural Nouns

Most nouns form their plural by adding –s to the noun.

Singular Noun	Plural Noun
computer	computers
tree	trees
Canadian	Canadians

Some nouns have spelling changes before adding –s.

Rule	Singular	Plural
If a noun ends in the letters s, sh, ch, or x, add –es to the noun.	brush box	brushes boxes
If a noun ends in a consonant plus y, change the y to i and add –es.	party baby	parties babies
For some nouns ending in f or fe, change the f to v and add –s. (Exceptions: belief—beliefs; chief—chief; roof—roofs.	leaf life	leaves lives

Some nouns have irregular plural forms.

Singular Noun	Plural Noun
man	men
woman	women
child	children
foot	feet
tooth	teeth
mouse	mice
fish	fish
deer	deer

Pronouns

Pronouns take the place of nouns.

> **Robert [n]** bought **a present [n]** for **his niece [n]**.
>
> **He [p]** gave **it [p]** to **her [p]**.

Subject Pronouns

	Singular	Plural	Singular Example	Plural Example
1st Person	I	we	**I** am late.	**We** are late.
2nd Person	you	you	**You** have enough time.	**You** all have enough time.
3rd Person	he, she, it	they	**He** was late, too.	**They** were late, too.

Object Pronouns

	Singular	Plural	Singular Example	Plural Example
1st Person	me	us	She likes **me**.	She likes all of **us**.
2nd Person	you	you	She doesn't like **you**.	She doesn't like any of **you**.
3rd Person	him, her it	them	I like **her**.	I like **them**.

Possessive Pronouns

	Singular	Plural	Singular Example	Plural Example
1st Person	mine	ours	That bag is **mine**.	Those bags are **ours**.
2nd Person	yours	yours	It's not **yours**.	The tickets are **yours**.
3rd Person	his, hers, its	theirs	It's **his**.	The bags over there are **theirs**.

Reflexive Pronouns

	Singular	Plural	Singular Example	Plural Example
1st Person	myself	ourselves	I cut **myself.**	We climbed that mountain **ourselves.**
2nd Person	yourself	yourselves	Did you hurt **yourself?**	Did all of you do the work **yourselves?**
3rd Person	himself herself itself	themselves	It turned **itself** off.	All the players put their bats away **themselves.**

Comparative and Superlative Adjective Forms

Comparative Adjectives

Adjectives that are used to compare two things have special forms. Sometimes we add *–er*. Sometimes we use *more* in front of the adjective. These forms are called comparative adjectives.

	Adjective	Comparative
One-syllable adjectives **Rule: add** *–er*	tall nice	taller nicer
Adjectives that end in *y* **Rule: change** *y* **to** *i* **and** **add** *–er*	pretty funny	prettier funnier
Adjectives with two or more **syllables** **Rule: use** *more*	beautiful interesting	**more** beautiful **more** interesting

Superlative Adjectives

Adjectives that are used to compare three or more things have special forms. Sometimes we add *–est*. Sometimes we use *most* in front of the adjective. These forms are called superlative adjectives.

	Adjective	Superlative
One syllable adjectives **Rule: add** *–est*	tall nice	the tallest (of many) the nicest (of all)
Adjectives that end in *y* **Rule: change** *y* **to** *i* **and** **add** *–est*	pretty funny	the prettiest the funniest
Adjectives with two syllables **Rule: Use** *most*	beautiful interesting	**the most** beautiful **the most** interesting

Irregular Comparatives and Superlatives

Adjective	Comparative	Superlative
good	better	best
bad	worse	worst
far	farther	farthest

Principal Parts of Verbs

All verbs except *to be* have three principal parts. You can make all other verb forms from those three parts.

	Example	Uses
Present	play	Simple present tense: *I play.* Add *–s* for third person singular: *He, she, it plays.*
		Infinitive: *to play*
		Present participle (add *–ing*): *playing*
		Gerund (add *–ing*): *playing*
Past	played	Simple past tense: *We played.*
Past participle	played	Present perfect tense: *They have played.*
		Past perfect tense: *They had played.*
		Perfect modals: *I could have played.*
		Passive voice: *It is played.*

Principal Parts of Regular Verbs

For most verbs, add *–ed* to the present form to make the past and past participle forms. Some verbs have special spelling rules for these forms.

Rule	Example
If a verb already ends in *e*, just add *–d*.	hope—hop**ed**
If a verb ends in a single vowel plus a single consonant, double the consonant and add *–ed*.	wrap—wrap**ped**
If a verb ends in a single consonant plus *y*, change the *y* to *i* and add *–ed*.	carry—carr**ied**

Irregular Verbs

To Be

Some important verbs do not follow standard rules. The most important of these is *to be*. *To be* is irregular in all of its principal parts.

	I	you	he, she, it	we	you	they
Present	am	are	is	are	are	are
Past	was	were	was	were	were	were
Past Participle	been	been	been	been	been	been

Has, Do, Go

Three verbs are irregular only in the third person singular of the present tense.

	I	you	he, she, it
have	have	have	has
do	do	do	does
go	go	go	goes

Common Irregular Verbs

Many common verbs are irregular in their past and past participle forms.

PRESENT	PAST	PAST PARTICIPLE	PRESENT	PAST	PAST PARTICIPLE
arise	arose	risen	grind	ground	ground
awake	awoke	awakened	grow	grew	grown
bear	bore	born	hang	hung	hung
beat	beat	beaten	have	had	had
become	became	become	hear	heard	heard
begin	began	begun	hide	hid	hidden
bend	bent	bent	hit	hit	hit
bet	bet	bet	hold	held	held
bind	bound	bound	hurt	hurt	hurt
bite	bit	bitten	keep	kept	kept
bleed	bled	bled	know	knew	known
blow	blew	blown	lay	laid	laid
break	broke	broken	lead	led	led
bring	brought	brought	leave	left	left
build	built	built	lend	lent	lent
burst	burst	burst	let	let	let
cast	cast	cast	lie	lay	lain
catch	caught	caught	light	lit	lit
choose	chose	chosen	lost	lost	lost
cling	clung	clung	make	made	made
come	came	come	mean	meant	meant
cost	cost	cost	pay	paid	paid
creep	crept	crept	read	read	read
cut	cut	cut	ride	rode	ridden
deal	dealt	dealt	ring	rang	rung
dig	dug	dug	rise	rose	risen
do	did	done	run	ran	run
draw	drew	drawn	see	saw	seen
dream	dreamed (dreamt)	dreamed (dreamt)	seek	sought	sought
			sell	sold	sold
drink	drank	drunk	send	sent	sent
drive	drove	driven	set	set	set
eat	ate	eaten	shake	shook	shaken
fall	fell	fallen	shave	shaved	shaven
feed	fed	fed	shine	shone	shone
feel	felt	felt	shoot	shot	shot
fight	fought	fought	show	showed	shown (showed)
find	found	found			
fling	flung	flung	shrink	shrank	shrunk
fly	flew	flown	shut	shut	shut
forget	forget	forgotten	sing	sang	sung
forgive	forgave	forgiven	sink	sank	sunk
freeze	froze	frozen	sit	sat	sat
get	got	gotten	sleep	slept	slept
give	gave	given	slide	slid	slid
go	went	gone	slit	slit	slit

Common Irregular Verbs

Present	Past	Past Participle	Present	Past	Past Participle
speak	spoke	spoken	teach	taught	taught
speed	sped	sped	tear	tore	torn
spend	spent	spent	tell	told	told
spin	spun	spun	think	thought	thought
split	split	split	throw	threw	thrown
spread	spread	spread	understand	understood	understood
spring	sprang	sprung	wake	woke	woke
stand	stood	stood	wear	wore	worn
steal	stole	stolen	weave	wove	woven
stick	stuck	stuck	wed	wed	wed
sting	stung	stung	weep	wept	wept
strike	struck	struck	wet	wet	wet
string	strung	strung	win	won	won
swear	swore	sworn	wind	wound	wound
sweep	swept	swept	wring	wrung	wrung
swim	swam	swum	write	wrote	written
take	took	taken			

Present Tenses

	Simple Present	Present Continuous	Present Perfect	Present Perfect Continuous
I	work.	am working.	have worked.	have been working.
You	work.	are working.	have worked.	have been working.
He She It	works.	is working.	has worked.	has been working.
We	work.	are working.	have worked.	have been working.
You	work.	are working.	have worked.	have been working.
They	work.	are working.	have worked.	have been working.

Past Tenses

	Simple Past	Past Continuous	Past Perfect	Past Perfect Continuous
I	worked.	was working.	had worked.	had been working.
You	worked.	were working.	had worked.	had been working.
He She It	worked.	is working.	had worked.	had been working.
We	worked.	were working.	had worked.	had been working.
You	worked.	were working.	had worked.	had been working.
They	worked.	were working.	had worked.	had been working.

Verb Tenses

Future Tenses

	Simple Future	Future Continuous	Future Perfect	Future Perfect Continuous
I	will work.	will be working.	will have worked.	will have been working.
You	will work.	will be working.	will have worked.	will have been working.
He She It	will work.	will be working.	will have worked.	will have been working.
We	will work.	will be working.	will have worked.	will have been working.
You	will work.	will be working.	will have worked.	will have been working.
They	will work.	will be working.	will have worked.	will have been working.

The present continuous and *going to* + verb also express the future.

Active and Passive Voice

Verbs that can take direct objects can be active or passive. Use the *active* voice when you are focusing on who did the action. Use the *passive voice* when you don't know who did the action, when it is not important to know who did the action, or when you are focusing on what was done rather than on the doer.

Active:	Pablo Picasso painted "Guernica" in 1937.
Passive:	"Guernica" was painted by Pablo Picasso in 1937.

Form the passive voice with *to be* in the same tense as the active verb and the past participle of the active verb.

Tense	Active Verb	Passive Verb
Simple Present	paint/paints	am/is/are painted
Present Continuous	am/is/are painting	am/is/are being painted
Present Perfect	has/have painted	has/have been painted
Present Perfect Continuous	have/has been painting	has/have been being painted
Simple Past	painted	was/were painted
Past Continuous	was/were painting	was/were being painted
Past Perfect	had painted	had been painted
Past Perfect Continuous	had been painting	had been being painted
Simple Future	will paint	will be painted
Future Continuous	will be painting	will be being painted
Future Perfect	will have painted	will have been painted
Future Perfect Continuous	will have been painting	will have been being painted

ANSWERS TO EXERCISES

PAGE 1

2. are 3. am 4. is 5. are 6. is 7. is 8. are 9. are 10. am 11. is 12. are 13. is 14. are 15. is 16. are

PAGE 2

A-B. 2. You are not angry.-Are you angry? 3. Ben and Liz are not cousins.-Are Ben and Liz cousins? 4. He is not very serious.-Is he very serious? 5. Both sisters are not tall.-Are both sisters tall? 6. She is not a clever woman.-Is she a clever woman? 7. They are not members of the country club.-Are they members of the country club? 8. He is not a good tennis player.-Is he a good tennis player? 9. Elaine is not a pilot with an international airline.-Is Elaine a pilot with an international airline? 10. The sky is not very cloudy today.-Is the sky very cloudy today? 11. The office of the supervisor is not on the first floor.-Is the office of the supervisor on the first floor? 12. It is not cold today.-Is it cold today? 13. She is not in her office.-Is she in her office? 14. The stamps are not in my desk.-Are the stamps in my desk? 15. He is not a smart man.-Is he a smart man?

PAGE 3

2. an 3. an 4. an 5. a, an 6. a 7. an 8. a 9. a 10. a 11. an 12. an 13. an 14. an 15. an 16. a 17. a 18. a

PAGE 4

A. salesmen, buzzes, oranges, dishes, glasses, players, feet
B. 2. The glasses are in the kitchen.
3. The dishes are new. 4. The buses are at the corner. 5. The children are in the garden. 6. The clocks are on the wall. 7. The watches are new. 8. The pictures are beautiful.

PAGE 5

2. knives 3. tomatoes 4. boys 5. shelves 6. volcanoes 7. leaves 8. toys 9. potatoes 10. thieves 11. keys 12. butterflies

PAGE 6

2. has 3. have 4. has 5. have 6. has 7. has 8. have 9. have 10. has 11. has 12. have 13. have 14. has 15. has 16. have 17. has 18. has 19. have 20. have

PAGE 7

2. come 3. walk 4. play 5. eat 6. works 7. like 8. chases 9. works 10. sits 11. play 12. cook 13. eat 14. ride 15. take 16. travel 17. attend 18. speaks

PAGE 8

2. does 3. try 4. tries 5. wishes 6. teaches 7. go 8. watch 9. plays 10. studies 11. watches 12. kisses 13. catch 14. catches 15. does 16. carries

PAGE 9

B-C-D. 2. He teaches science at a high school. They teach science at a high school. She teaches science at a high school. 3. He works hard. They work hard. She works hard. 4. He owns a-They own a-She owns a 5. He lives in-They live in-She lives in 6. He enjoys each-They enjoy each-She enjoys each 7. He wants to-They want to -She wants to 8. He has a new wristwatch. They have new wristwatches. She has a new wristwatch. 9. He speaks-They speak-She speaks 10. He wishes to-They wish to-She wishes to 11. He reads-They read-She reads 12. He passes-They pass-She passes 13. He always goes-They always go-She always goes 14. He tries-They try-She tries 15. He does-They do-She does 16. He plays-They play-She plays 17. He has-They have-She has 18. He always sits at this desk. They always sit at these desks. She always sits at this desk. 19. He does his-They do their-She does her 20. He studies-They study-She studies

PAGE 10

2. my 3. her 4. my 5. your 6. their 7. his 8. our 9. her 10. its, its 11. their 12. my 13. its 14. their 15. your 16. our 17. her

PAGE 11

2. There is 3. There are 4. There is 5. There are 6. There are 7. There is 8. There are 9. There is 10. There is 11. There are 12. There are 13. There is 14. There is 15. There are 16. There are

PAGE 12

A-B. 2. There aren't two-Are there two 3. There isn't a-Is there a 4. There aren't two-Are there two 5. There isn't a-Is there a 6. There aren't many-Are there many 7. There aren't ten new-Are there ten new-8. There isn't a-Is there a 9. There aren't enough-Are there enough 10. There isn't a-Is there 11. There isn't a-Is there 12. There aren't telephones-Are there telephones

PAGE 13

2. Laura's 3. Chicago's 4. men's 5. ladies' 6. child's 7. children's 8. Bob's 9. doctor's 10. Lincoln's 11. Sally's 12. Jackson's 13. St. Peter's, St. Paul's

Page 14

2. These rooms are 3. Those pens. . . are 4. These stacks. . . belong 5. Those boys. . . are. . . brothers 6. Those books are 7. Those purses. . . are 8. These are. . . chairs 9. Those are. . . pens 10. These messages are 11. Those letters. . . are 12. These are my pens 13. Those mountains. . . form 14. These cars belong 15. Those offices. . . are. . . offices 16. These chairs are

Page 15

A. 2. us 3. her 4. us 5. me 6. them 7. him 8. him 9. us 10. me 11. us 12. them 13. her 14. me 15. her 16. us 17. her 18. me 19. me 20. them

Page 16

B. 2. them 3. her 4. you 5. them 6. them 7. us 8. them 9. him 10. her 11. them 12. him 13. him or her 14. him or her 15. her 16. them 17. him 18. them 19. them 20. them

Page 17

A-B-C. 2. Give this-Don't give this-Please give this 3. Open-Don't open-Please open 4. Close-Don't close-Please close 5. Wait-Don't wait-Please wait 6. Call-Don't call-Please call 7. Let-Don't let-Please let 8. Let-Don't let-Please let 9. Turn off-Don't turn off-Please turn off 10. Put-Don't put-Please put 11. Drop-Don't drop-Please drop 12. Leave-Don't leave-Please leave 13. Let-Don't let-Please let 14. Help-Don't help-Please help 15. Send-Don't send-Please send

Page 19

2. Ella does not like-Ella doesn't like 3. You do not speak-You don't speak 4. The plane does not leave-The plane doesn't leave 5. He does not know-He doesn't know 6. I do not feel-I don't feel 7. He does not eat-He doesn't eat 8. She does not always come-She doesn't always come 9. They do not live-They don't live 10. We do not need-We don't need 11. Janet and I do not cook-Janet and I don't cook 12. I do not understand-I don't understand 13. She does not want-She doesn't want 14. He does not begin-He doesn't begin 15. My son does not play-My son doesn't play 16. Gina and James do not make-Gina and James don't make

Page 20

2. Do they enjoy 3. Does that company buy 4. Does it look 5. Does he drive 6. Does the committee meet 7. Does he seem to be 8. Does this

book belong 9. Do you like 10. Do you speak 11. Does he often go 12. Do I take 13. Do they sell 14. Does the store open 15. Does it close 16. Does he eat

Page 21

A. 2. do 3. does 4. does 5. do 6. does 7. do 8. does 9. do 10. does 11. does 12. do 13. does 14. does 15. do 16. do 17. does 18. do 19. do 20. do 21. does 22. do

Page 22

B. 2. What time does the play begin? 3. When do they get home every night? 4. How well does the travel agent speak French? 5. How much do those books cost? 6. How do they travel? 7. How often does he come here? 8. How does she feel? 9. Why does Francine want to learn English? 10. Where do they meet every morning? 11. How often do we go to the movies? 12. Where do the children go after lunch? 13. How many new words do we learn every day? 14. Where do they eat lunch? 15. What kind of car does he drive? 16. Where does this plate belong? 17. Where does the committee meet? 18. What does she teach us? 19. When does it rain? 20. What time does he get up every morning? 21. When does she go to bed?

Page 23

2. was 3. were 4. was 5. were 6. was 7. were 8. were 9. were 10. was 11. were 12. was, was 13. was 14. were 15. were 16. were 17. were 18. was

Page 24

A-B. 2. These doors were not-These doors weren't-Were these doors closed? 3. The exercises were not-The exercises weren't-Were the exercises easy to do? 4. The man was not-The man wasn't-Was the man a stranger to her? 5. It was not-It wasn't-Was it a pleasant day? 6. The sea was not-The sea wasn't-Was the sea very rough? 7. He was not-He wasn't-Was he a tall man? 8. There were not-There weren't-Were there ten new words in the lesson? 9. Sarah was not-Sarah wasn't-Was Sarah a good swimmer? 10. She was not-She wasn't-Was she very intelligent? 11. They were not-They weren't-Were they both Americans? 12. She was not-She wasn't-Was she a good tennis player? 13. You were not-You weren't-Were you a happy child? 14. He was not-He wasn't-Was he always angry? 15. They were not-They weren't-Were they friendly enemies? 16. Bert was not-Bert wasn't-Was Bert an old friend of the family?

PAGE 26

2. listened 3. talked 4. wanted 5. lived 6. expected 7. lasted 8. changed 9. liked 10. waited 11. painted 12. arrived 13. watched 14. studied 15. mailed

PAGE 27

B. 2. told 3. sat 4. put 5. began 6. wrote 7. saw 8. cost 9. ate 10. drank 11. gave, told 12. sold 13. heard 14. knew, came 15. felt 16. went, got 17. read 18. had 19. spoke

PAGE 28

D. 2. brought 3. forgot 4. became 5. made 6. lost, found 7. fought 8. rang 9. sent 10. thought 11. taught 12. bought, sold 13. kept, gave 14. did, caught 15. sang, understood 16. stood 17. broke, took

PAGE 29

F. 2. paid 3. shook, said 4. blew 5. threw, hit 6. slept 7. met 8. found 9. wore 10. cut, ran 11. drove 12. held 13. won, lost 14. shut, went 15. rode

PAGE 31

2. You did not tell-You didn't tell 3. He did not put-He didn't put 4. They did not stay-They didn't stay 5. Judy and I did not see-Judy and I didn't see 6. He did not plan-He didn't plan 7. The meeting did not last-The meeting didn't last 8. The book did not cost-The book didn't cost 9. Gina and her husband did not work-Gina and her husband didn't work 10. I did not know-I didn't know 11. They did not sell-They didn't sell 12. I did not speak-I didn't speak 13. She did not come-She didn't come 14. We did not sit-We didn't sit 15. I did not go-I didn't go 16. You did not give-You didn't give

PAGE 32

2. Did he give 3. Did they stay 4. Did she tell 5. Did you move 6. Did Terry fly 7. Did we go 8. Did they come 9. Did Carla and Dave know 10. Did he work 11. Did she feel 12. Did the meeting begin 13. Did I pass 14. Did they put 15. Did I give 16. Did the crowd wait

PAGE 33

2. When did they sell their home? 3. What time did the meeting begin? 4. How much did the tickets cost? 5. How did he pay for the car? 6. How much did she invest in the stock market? 7. Where did they sit? 8. When did he speak to them? 9. How long did the meeting last? 10. What time did it begin? 11. What time did I call her? 12. Why did he go to Denver? 13. How many times did you mention it to him? 14. Where did they eat lunch? 15. How many years did we work there? 16. Where did I put the mail? 17. How long did she wait for them? 18. What time did we get home? 19. Who did he walk to the meeting with? 20. Where did you go after the lesson?

PAGE 34

A-B-C. 2. There are not eleven-There aren't eleven-Are there eleven-How many months are there in a year? 3. The plane did not arrive-The plane didn't arrive-Did the plane arrive-When did the plane arrive? 4. It is not-It isn't-Is it-What time is it now? 5. He did not go-He didn't go-Did he go-How did he go to Chicago? 6. The two boys are not-The two boys aren't-Are the two boys-Where are the two boys? 7. The magazine did not cost-The magazine didn't cost-Did the magazine cost-How much did the magazine cost? 8. They do not live-They don't live-Do they live-Where do they live now? 9. They did not live-They didn't live-Did they live-How long did they live in France? 10. He did not get up-He didn't get up-Did he get up-What time did he get up this morning? 11. They did not sit-They didn't sit-Did they sit-How long did they sit in the park? 12. She does not speak-She doesn't speak-Does she speak-What language does she speak? 13. The meeting does not begin-The meeting doesn't begin-Does the meeting begin-What time does the meeting begin? 14. She does not drink-She doesn't drink-Does she drink-How many cups of coffee does she drink every day? 15. They did not begin-They didn't begin-Did they begin-When did they begin to work? 16. I am not-I'm not-Am I-How old am I? 17. They do not plan-They don't plan-Do they plan-When do they plan to finish the work? 18. We did not get-We didn't get-Did we get-When did we get sick? 19. The stores were not closed-The stores weren't closed-Were the stores closed-Why were the stores closed?

PAGE 35

2. wrote 3. forgot 4. arrived 5. answered 6. made 7. rang 8. waited 9. went, rang 10. cost 11. tried 12. had 13. planned 14. took 15. sent 16. needed, bought 17. spoke 18. told, had 19. broke

PAGE 36

A. 2. She brought me the magazines. 3. She sent them flowers. 4. He told us the whole story. 5. I cooked Victoria dinner. 6. We wrote them several letters. 7. I took her the presents. 8. He sold a friend his property. 9. He gave each child a piece of the candy. 10. Don't show anyone these pictures. 11. He bought his wife several new dresses. 12. They sent us some postcards from South America.

B. 2. I sent many presents to her. 3. Please hand that magazine to me. 4. Don't tell the news to her yet. 5. You made a sweater for your sister. 6. Don't show these things to Flo. 7. He wrote a letter to me on Wednesday. 8. She told the whole story to us. 9. The teacher gives a lot of homework to us. 10. You made a promise to me that you must keep.

PAGE 38

2. that 3. who 4. who 5. which 6. whom 7. whom 8. that 9. that 10. that 11. which 12. who 13. who 14. that

PAGE 39

2. They will-They'll see 3. They will be happy-They'll be happy 4. She will-She'll help 5. Mary will-Mary'll clean off 6. The stores will-The stores'll close 7. I will-I'll leave 8. Helen will-Helen'll find 9. You will-You'll spend 10. Ms. Koboski will-Ms. Koboski'll be 11. The wind will-The wind'll blow 12. We will-We'll meet 13. I will-I'll pay 14. You will-You'll learn 15. We will-We'll remain 16. We will-We'll be tired 17. I will-I'll give 18. John will-John'll do

PAGE 40

2. We will not tell-We won't tell 3. I will not be-I won't be 4. The weather will not be-The weather won't be 5. He will not be able to meet-He won't be able to meet 6. These exercises will not be-These exercises won't be 7. We will not eat-We won't eat 8. You will not get tired-You won't get tired 9. We will not be there-We won't be there 10. I will not do-I won't do 11. They will not sign-They won't sign 12. They will not finish-They won't finish 13. The meeting will not last-The meeting won't last 14. The stores will not close-The stores won't close 15. It will not cost-It won't cost 16. We will not be ready-We won't be ready

PAGE 41

A-B. 2. Will I be back-When will I be back? 3. Will the stores be-How late will the stores be open? 4. Will it cost-How much will it cost to fix the computer? 5. Will the plant die-Why will the plant die? 6. Will they spend-How much time will they spend in France? 7. Will she meet us-Where will she meet us? 8. Will they pay-When will they pay their bill? 9. Will the meeting begin-When will the meeting begin? 10. Will it last-How long will it last? 11. Will she leave a-What will she leave on the table for him? 12. Will you return-When will you return? 13. Will there be-How many new members will there be in the club? 14. Will the meeting be-When will the

meeting be over? 15. Will they write to us-When will they write to us?

PAGE 42

Answers will vary.

PAGE 43

2. It took me an hour to finish my work. 3. It took her only one year to learn to speak English well. 4. It took me thirty minutes to write my paper. 5. It took the train three hours to go around the mountain. 6. It took them one year to finish the bridge. 7. It took the package two days to reach him. 8. It takes us about fifteen minutes to walk to school every morning. 9. It will take you about an hour to get there. 10. It will take us two hours to paint the bathroom. 11. It'll take you only one and one-half hours to paint the kitchen. 12. It takes me less than fifteen minutes to wash and dress each morning. 13. It takes the clown half an hour to put on his makeup. 14. It took him just a few days to learn to swim. 15. It took her two months to recover from her illness. 16. It will take me just two or three minutes to run to the corner store and get what you need.

PAGE 44

2. is stopping 3. is ringing 4. are wearing 5. is beginning 6. is knocking 7. is sleeping 8. is trying 9. is doing 10. are beginning 11. is having 12. is playing 13. are traveling 14. is acting 15. are having

PAGE 45

2. meets 3. is teaching-is substituting 4. rings-is ringing 5. is watching-watches 6. is knocking 7. comes 8. am reading 9. blows 10. is acting 11. is having 12. is studying 13. get 14. stays-comes-is staying 15. rises-is rising 16. are building

PAGE 46

A-B. 2. It is not beginning-It isn't beginning-Is it beginning 3. The sky is not getting-The sky isn't getting-Is the sky getting 4. She is not working-She isn't working-Is she working 5. The maid is not cleaning-The maid isn't cleaning-Is the maid cleaning 6. They are not taking-They aren't taking-Are they taking 7. You are not having-You aren't having-Are you having 8. John is not doing-John isn't doing-Is John doing 9. We are not laughing-We aren't laughing-Are we laughing 10. They are not traveling-They aren't traveling-Are they traveling 11. I am not taking-I'm not taking-Am I taking 12. The leaves are not beginning-The leaves

ANSWERS TO EXERCISES

aren't beginning-Are the leaves beginning
13. All the birds are not flying-All the birds aren't flying-Are all the birds flying 14. Ellen is not writing-Ellen isn't writing-Is Ellen writing

PAGE 47

2. They're 3. I'll 4. She's 5. It's 6. She'll 7. We're 8. They're 9. It's 10. We're 11. You'll 12. It's 13. There's 14. They'll

PAGE 48

2. They don't 3. She isn't 4. He isn't 5. They aren't 6. He doesn't 7. You didn't 8. She doesn't 9. You aren't 10. We weren't 11. George wasn't 12. She and her husband don't 13. I won't 14. There weren't 15. They won't 16. You aren't 17. There aren't

PAGE 49

2. a 3. a 4. The 5. a 6. The 7. The 8. A

PAGE 51

A. 2.- 3. The 4. the, the 5. the 6.-, -7.- 8.- 9. The 10. The 11. -, the, the 12. the 13. the -, -, -, - 14. -, a, - 15. -, -, the, - 16. The, the 17. - 18. The, the 19. - 20. the, the 21. - 22. the

PAGE 52

B. 2.-, the 3. the (a), the, 4. the, the 5. The, - 6. -, the, the, -7. The, the, -, -8. The, -9.-, -, the 10. The 11. The, the, the, the 12. The, -13. -, - 14. The, -, the 15. The 16. The, a 17. The, -

C. 2. The, the, the 3. a, a, a, a, the 4. the (a) -5. the, -, -, - 6. a, the 7. The, -, the -, 8. the, the, -, 9. - , The 10. - 11. the, the 12. The, the 13. the, The 14.-, the 15.-,-,-,-,- 16.-

PAGE 54

2. We are going to eat-We're going to eat 3. I am going to leave-I'm going to leave 4. They are going to wait-They're going to wait 5. We are going to get up-We're going to get up 6. She is going to drive-She's going to drive 7. We are going to go-We're going to go 8. You are going to have-You're going to have 9. They are going to go-They're going to go 10. Mike is going to take-Mike's going to take 11. It is going to be-It's going to be 12. it is going to rain-it's going to rain 13. Henry is going to study-Henry's going to study 14. You are going to stay-You're going to stay 15. Mr. and Mrs. Blake are going to build-Mr. and Mrs. Blake're going to build 16. He is going to start-He's going to start 17. They are going to move-They're going to move

PAGE 55

2. We were going (We were going to go) 3. I was going to 4. They were going to 5. We were going (We were going to go) 6. You were going to 7. They were going to 8. he was going to 9. I was going to 10. I was going to 11. They were going to 12. she was going to 13. We were going (We were going to go) 14. I was going to

PAGE 56

2. is coming 3. are-going-is-going 4. is flying 5. is-coming 6. is-leaving 7. am going 8. is arriving 9. are-going-Is-going 10. is leaving 11. are coming 12. is going-is-going 13. is-arriving 14. is coming 15. is flying 16. am leaving 17. is-leaving

PAGE 57

2. You may not 3. We should not, We shouldn't 4. He may not 5. They cannot, They can't 6. We must not, We mustn't 7. I cannot, I can't 8. She should not, She shouldn't 9. We must not, We mustn't 10. She cannot, She can't 11. He cannot, He can't 12. You should not, You shouldn't 13. She may not 14. You cannot, You can't 15. You may not

PAGE 58

2. Can they both speak English well? 3. Should Betsy spend more time on her English? 4. May we sit in these chairs? 5. Can they meet us at two o'clock? 6. May I call you later? 7. Should he eat less meat? 8. May he tell her? 9. Should we speak to her about it? 10. May they leave now? 11. Could you go by plane? 12. Could you send them a fax? 13. Should I stay at home more? 14. May Allan wait in his office? 15. Can Al go with us to the beach? 16. Could she leave immediately?

PAGE 59

2. Where could the babysitter wait? 3. Where may you study? 4. Where can you eat? 5. How well can I understand English? 6. What time should you be here? 7. What should we tell her about? 8. Where can he meet us? 9. When must the children come home? 10. Where can they hang their coats? 11. What should I tell her? 12. What time must you be here? 13. Where should Karen sit? 14. What time should we finish this? 15. How many languages can Gabriel speak? 16. What must you do first?

PAGE 60

A-B. 2. Yes, I do. No, I don't. 3. Yes, he/she does. No, he/she doesn't. 4. Yes, he/she does. No, he/she doesn't. 5. Yes, I will. No, I won't. 6. Yes, he will. No, he won't. 7. Yes, I am. No, I'm not. 8. Yes, it is. No, it isn't. 9. Yes, it does. No, it doesn't. 10. Yes, it is. No, it isn't. 11. Yes, it is. No, it isn't. 12. Yes, I did. No, I didn't. 13. Yes, I did. No, I didn't. 14. Yes, it is. No, it isn't. 15. Yes, it was. No, it wasn't. 16. Yes, he/she did. No, he/she didn't. 17. Yes, it is. No, it isn't. 18. Yes, it was. No, it wasn't. 19. Yes, it will. No, it won't. 20. Yes, you may. No, you may not. 21. Yes, I can. No, I can't. 22. Yes, it did. No, it didn't. 23. Yes, I did. No, I didn't. 24. Yes, I was. No, I wasn't. 25. Yes, I will. No, I won't. 26. Yes, it is. No, it isn't.

PAGE 62

2. hard 3. quickly 4. slowly 5. slowly 6. slow 7. rapidly 8. permanent 9. permanently 10. easy 11. easily 12. hard 13. fast 14. serious 15. seriously 16. completely 17. soft 18. softly 19. beautiful 20. beautifully

PAGE 64

2. well 3. good 4. well 5. good 6. good 7. well 8. Well 9. well 10. good 11. well, good 12. good 13. well 14. good 15. good 16. well 17. good 18. well 19. well 20. good 21. well 22. good

PAGE 66

A. 2. older than 3. bigger than 4. better than 5. worse than 6. more difficult than 7. more valuable than 8. more attractive than 9. more often than 10. more frequently than 11. later than

PAGE 67

B. 2. more carefully than 3. harder than 4. longer than 5. more bravely than 6. more quickly than 7. more loudly than 8. sooner than 9. warmer than 10. more expensive than 11. more satisfactory than 12. wider than 13. more complicated than 14. better than 15. cleverer than 16. hotter than 17. more fluently than

PAGE 68

2. the most expensive 3. the worst 4. the most important 5. the hardest 6. the most ambitious 7. the latest 8. the most gracefully 9. the most intelligent 10. the saddest 11. the coldest 12. the best

PAGE 70

A. 2. was raining 3. was having 4. were traveling 5. sleeping 6. was just ordering 7. were driving 8. was working 9. was just taking 10. was talking 11. were traveling 12. was getting 13. was traveling

PAGE 71

B. 3. I was going 4. I went 5. We drove 6. We were driving 7. We were having 8. We had 9. I was coming 10. I came 11. wind was blowing 12. wind blew 13. It rained 14. It was raining 15. sun was shining 16. sun shone 17. I was reading 18. I read 19. I was sleeping 20. I slept 21. June was playing

C. 2. was raining-left 3. fell-hurt-was riding 4. called-were having 5. was driving-heard 6. were sitting-drove 7. was getting out-slipped-broke 8. was driving-happened 9. came-was leaving 10. were leaving-dropped 11. was talking-saw 12. telephoned-was working

PAGE 72

D. Answers will vary. 2. I was talking 3. Tony was walking 4. She was eating 5. I was finishing 6. Larry was speaking 7. I was writing 8. He was living 9. They were getting off 10. We were having 11. Chris was leaving 12. Dr. Berger was having 13. Sharon was typing 14. I was visiting 15. The puppy was crying

PAGE 73

2. will be traveling 3. will be having 4. will be waiting 5. will be practicing 6. will be raining 7. will be working 8. will be flying 9. will be watching 10. will be taking 11. will be studying

PAGE 74

A. 2. much 3. many 4. much 5. much 6. much 7. many 8. many 9. much 10. much 11. many 12. many 13. much 14. many

B. Sentences 2, 3, 4, 5, 6, 7, 8, 9, 14

PAGE 76

A. 2. John doesn't like to play tennis either. 3. They don't want to move to the suburbs either. 4. Richard won't come either. 5. He doesn't eat in that restaurant either. 6. We can't play baseball either. 7. He doesn't like American food either. 8. She isn't able to hear him either. 9. My parents don't like to listen to the radio either. 10. Mr. Johnson isn't a tennis player either. 11. Molly can't play this game either. 12. This book wasn't expensive either.

B. 2. She also likes to watch television.-She likes to watch television too. 3. Helen can also swim well.-Helen can swim well too. 4. The manager was also able to speak to him.-The manager was able to speak to him too. 5. They also want to live in the suburbs.-They want to live in the suburbs too. 6. My sister will also be back before noon.-My sister will be back before noon too. 7. He also comes to work by bus.-He comes to work by bus too. 8. Rachel is also a friendly person.-Rachel is a friendly person too.

PAGE 78

A. 2. We didn't see any good 3. He didn't make any mistakes 4. They don't have any pretty 5. The teacher didn't teach us any important 6. We didn't learn any new 7. There aren't any flowers 8. There aren't any rich 9. We don't have any good

B. 2. Pour me some coffee. 3. We need some more chairs in this room. 4. There are some tables in the hall. 5. She wants some oranges. 6. They told us about some of their experiences. 7. There are some good seats left for the play tonight. 8. You'll need some winter clothes in San Diego. 9. I have some more money.

PAGE 79

C. 2. some 3. any 4. any 5. some 6. any 7. any 8. any 9. some-any 10. any-some 11. some 12. any 13. any 14. some 15. some-any 16. any 17. any-any 18. any 19. some 20. any 21. any 22. some-any 23. any 24. some

PAGE 80

A. 2. There isn't anyone at the door. 3. You didn't leave anything on the hall table. 4. Bob won't bring anyone with him. 5. I didn't lose the book anywhere downtown. 6. There isn't anybody in the next room. 7. Bobbie didn't go anywhere last night with her boss. 8. He doesn't have anything important to say to you.

B. 2. There is something wrong with Toby's ear. 3. There was someone at the door. 4. We have spoken to somebody about it. 5. There does seem to be somebody in the office. 6. My keys are somewhere in this room. 7. I think there is something wrong with the printer. 8. They found her somewhere.

PAGE 81

A. 2. ours 3. hers 4. yours 5. his 6. his 7. yours, mine 8. hers, mine 9. yours 10. yours 11. hers 12. theirs-ours 13. yours-mine 14. mine 15. mine 16. ours 17. mine 18. yours

PAGE 82

B. 3. is hers 4. is mine 5. is Adrian's 6. is Miss Jefferson's 7. are theirs 8. are ours 9. are theirs 10. isn't mine 11. is his 12. is Mrs. Jones' 13. is Robert's 14. are ours-are theirs 15. is mine-is yours

16. must be his 17. is the teacher's 18. are theirs 19. is our landlord's 20. isn't mine-is my father's 21. is mine-is Virginia's 22. is Jim's little brother's

PAGE 83

C. 2. my-hers 3. their-ours 4. our-theirs 5. my-his 6. their-ours 7. my-yours 8. his-hers 9. his-yours 10. their-ours 11. my-hers 12. my-hers 13. our-theirs 14. his-mine 15. his or her-his or her 16. my-hers 17. our-theirs 18. your-mine 19. their-ours 20. our-theirs

PAGE 84

2. ourselves 3. himself 4. themselves 5. ourselves 6. themselves 7. herself 8. yourself (yourselves) 9. yourself (yourselves) 10. myself 11. myself 12. herself 13. himself 14. herself 15. herself 16. itself

PAGE 85

2. myself 3. herself 4. himself 5. ourselves 6. herself (himself) 7. herself 8. myself 9. themselves 10. himself (herself) 11. themselves 12. himself (herself) 13. myself 14. yourself 15. themselves 16. himself 17. themselves 18. yourself (yourselves) 19. herself 20. myself

PAGE 86

2. by themselves 3. by myself 4. by herself (by himself) 5. by himself 6. by himself 7. by himself 8. by herself 9. by yourself (yourselves) 10. by myself 11. by themselves-by themselves 12. by oneself 13. by herself 14. by myself 15. by himself 16. by itself 17. by himself 18. by itself 19. by ourselves 20. by yourself (yourselves)

PAGE 87

2. have finished 3. has visited 4. has returned 5. have lost 6. have been 7. has rained 8. have learned 9. have told 10. have heard 11. have lent 12. has gone

PAGE 88

2. went 3. have read 4. read 5. have been 6. has had 7. fell 8. saw 9. jumped, ran 10. have tried 11. went 12. have completed

PAGE 89

2. lived 3. worked 4. has worked 5. studied 6. have studied 7. has spoken 8. worked 9. has worked 10. left, has worked 11. has studied 12. have studied 13. has been 14. felt

2. They have been talking 3. I have been traveling 4. He has been sleeping 5. It has been raining 6. He has been studying 7. We have been using 8. She has been teaching 9. They have been living 10. The two nations have been quarreling 11. She has been taking 12. They have been looking 13. He has been doing 14. Lynn has been working 15. You have been arguing

A-B. 2. She has not been teaching-She hasn't been teaching-Has she been teaching 3. It has not been snowing-It hasn't been snowing-Has it been snowing 4. I have not spoken to-I haven't spoken to-Have I spoken to 5. You have not been studying-You haven't been studying-Have you been studying 6. He has not been-He hasn't been-Has he been 7. She has not been taking-She hasn't been taking-Has she been taking 8. They have not been discussing-They haven't been discussing-Have they been discussing 9. She has not been-She hasn't been-Has she been 10. They have not returned-They haven't returned-Have they returned 11. He has not known-He hasn't known-Has he known 12. Joel has not found-Joel hasn't found-Has Joel found 13. You have not been-You haven't been-Have you been 14. He has not told-He hasn't told-Has he told 15. Garvin has not left-Garvin hasn't left-Has Garvin left 16. They have not been having-They haven't been having-Have they been having 17. He has not been feeling-He hasn't been feeling-Has he been feeling 18. They have not been married-They haven't been married-Have they been married

2. How long have they been 3. How long have they been 4. How long has he been 5. How long has she been 6. How long have they been 7. How long have they been 8. How long has he been 9. How long has it been 10. How long has she been 11. How long has he been 12. How long have they occupied 13. How long has he been 14. How long has she been 15. How long have they been 16. How long has the dog been 17. How long has he been 18. How long has she been

A. Answers will vary. 2. since 2000 3. since June 4. since Wednesday 5. since Tuesday 6. since last year 7. since seven o'clock 8. since 2001 9. since one o'clock 10. since June

B. Answers will vary. 2. for two months 3. for one year 4. for many years 5. for twelve hours 6. for many years 7. for six years 8. for a week 9. for three days 10. for six months

A. 2. already 3. yet (already)-yet 4. already 5. already 6. already 7. yet 8. yet (already) 9. yet (already)-yet 10. yet (already) 11. yet 12. already

B-C. 2. No, the mail hasn't arrived yet.-Yes, the mail has already arrived. 3. No, I haven't finished my homework yet.-Yes, I have already finished my homework. 4. No, Mr. Dole hasn't returned from lunch yet.-Yes, Mr. Dole has already returned from lunch. 5. No, I haven't paid that bill yet.-Yes, I have already paid that bill. 6. No, the meeting hasn't begun yet .-Yes, the meeting has already begun. 7. No, George hasn't found a job yet.-Yes, George has already found a job. 8. No, the boat hasn't sailed yet.-Yes, the boat has already sailed. 9. No, I haven't bought the tickets for the game yet.-Yes, I have already bought the tickets for the game. 10. No, I haven't ridden in Pam's new car yet-Yes, I have already ridden in Pam's new car.

A. 2. told 3. told 4. told-said 5. tell-said 6. said 7. told 8. told-tell 9. told 10. tell 11. told-said 12. said 13. Tell-said-said 14. tells-tell 15. said 16. told 17. told 18. tell 19. said 20. told 21. said 22. told 23. told 24. told 25. tell 26. told

B. 2. Gene told me that 3. She told me that 4. Joseph told me that 5. George told me that 6. I told him that 7. The student told me that 8. The man told me that 9. The stockbroker told me that 10. The man told me that 11. He also told me that 12. Jean told me that

C. 2. She said that 3. I said that 4. We said that 5. The manager said that 6. The doctor said that 7. He said that 8. I said that 9. We said that 10. I said that 11. He said that 12. I said that

2. had left 3. had captured 4. had gone 5. had taken 6. had made 7. had met 8. had left 9. had happened 10. had been 11. had given 12. had prepared 13. had done 14. had had 15. had seen

2. as large as 3. as wide as 4. so intelligent as 5. as early as 6. as beautifully as 7. as quickly as 8. as fast as 9. as well as 10. as carefully as 11. as regularly as 12. as early as 13. as easily as 14. as hard as 15. as soon as 16. as cold today as 17. so good as 18. as often as

PAGE 103

A. 2. She said she could not do 3. She said her name was Smith. 4. I thought I could finish 5. predicted that it would rain 6. Mr. Wik said he was very 7. complained that she had a 8. He thought he might finish 9. I did not think I could complete 10. promised that the error would not occur 11. He said the mail would certainly be 12. students thought they were making 13. They said the weather would probably be 14. I thought it would rain 15. He hoped he could get 16. I didn't think I would see 17. She said she might be 18. I thought he was out 19. Did he say she couldn't do 20. He complained that nobody believed a word he said. 21. I was certain. . . would go 22. She told me that prices were sure 23. promised faithfully that he would deliver 24. He hoped he might reach 25. He said that he had known 26. She said she had lived 27. She thought she could get 28. He said he was taking 29. declared that the prisoner wasn't guilty 30. They felt sure the battle would be 31. I wondered what. . . chairman would introduce 32. He swore he had never seen

PAGE 104

B. 2. They think they have found. . . they are mistaken. 3. He thinks the mail will surely be 4. The paper says it will rain 5. She says her name is 6. He says that he is too 7. I do not think he can finish 8. He says he'll be 9. I do not think she'll come. 10. Does he say he'll call 11. She promises she'll try to do 12. He tells me he thinks prices are going 13. He says he has found 14. She says she can't understand what I mean.

PAGE 106

A. 3. Len may be 4. Loretta may lend 5. She may call 6. Frank may offer 7. The weather may get 8. She may be 9. You may feel 10. It may not rain 11. We may be 12. He may not want 13. They may go 14. They may go

B. 2. He may pass all his examinations. I'm not sure. 3. He may be back 4. She may drive 5. We may be going 6. We may be going 7. She may wait 8. We may see 9. She may lend 10. They may take

PAGE 108

A-B. 2. They shouldn't make-They ought not to make 3. I should spend-I ought to spend 4. He shouldn't eat-He ought not to eat 5. You should learn-You ought to learn 6. You should ask-You ought to ask 7. He should get-He ought to get 8. You really should go-You really ought to go 9. Someone should tell-Someone ought to tell 10. No one should spend-No one ought to spend 11. She shouldn't waste-She ought not to waste

12. I should write-I ought to write 13. You shouldn't work-You ought not to work 14. You should rest-You ought to rest 15. We should pay-We ought to pay

PAGE 109

2. They have to stay there 3. You have to mail 4. He has to have more practice 5. They have to help her 6. You have to speak 7. He has to spend 8. You have to write 9. We have to leave 10. We have to learn 11. I have to take 12. You have to insure 13. Roger has to give 14. They have to spend 15. You have to pay 16. You have to help

PAGE 110

A-B. Answers will vary. 2. She had to have-She will have to have 3. Boris had to have-Boris will have to have 4. Everyone had to work-Everyone will have to work 5. He had to learn-He'll have to learn 6. I had to go-I'll have to go 7. She had to return-She'll have to return 8. He had to see-He'll have to see 9. We had to lend-We'll have to lend 10. You had to spend-You'll have to spend 11. They had to leave-They'll have to leave 12. We had to stay-We'll have to stay 13. You had to send-You'll have to send 14. He had to give-He'll have to give

PAGE 111

A-B. 2. They won't have to buy-Will they have to buy 3. I don't have to cash-Do I have to cash 4. He didn't have to pay-Did he have to pay 5. They didn't have to go-Did they have to go 6. She doesn't have to take-Does she have to take 7. He doesn't have to write-Does he have to write 8. We won't have to take-Will we have to take 9. They didn't have to wait-Did they have to wait 10. They don't have to learn-Do they have to learn 11. I don't have to go-Do I have to go 12. We didn't have to wait-Did we have to wait

PAGE 112

2. How long did they have to wait there? 3. Why did the children have to stay indoors? 4. Why did they have to leave the party early? 5. When does he have to go to Denver? 6. How long will he have to stay there? 7. How much did they have to pay for their medicine? 8. When do I have to go to the dentist again? 9. What time will you have to come back? 10. Why does he have to go to the post office? 11. How many new words does each student have to learn every day? 12. How often does she have to go there? 13. How much did they have to leave as a deposit? 14. What time does he have to leave? 15. Where do you have to sign your name? 16. Why does Mary have to do all the housework? 17. Whom shall I have to ask for the money?

PAGE 113

A. 2. for-in 3. in 4. for-in 5. for 6. at 7. in 8. into 9. of-on 10. about-in 11. to 12. to-for 13. in-of 14. along 15. at 16. at 17. for-in 18. for 19. on 20. about-to 21. at-about 22. in

PAGE 114

B. 2. on 3. into (through) 4. out 5. in 6. from 7. of 8. into 9. on (in) 10. at-in 11. in-at 12. from 13. on 14. in 15. at-of 16. in-of 17. beside (next to, with) 18. at-in 19. out 20. over 21. at-of 22. under (off)-across (onto) 23. to 24. at-in 25. down (through)-in (at)

PAGE 115

C. 2. by (at) 3. for 4. since 5. for 6. since 7. until (till, at) 8. for 9. in-At 10. in-to 11. for 12. at-at 13. in (for) 14. at (by)-of 15. by 16. from-to 17. in-to 18. from-to 19. during 20. at 21. in 22. in 23. at-at 24. since

PAGE 116

D. 2. with 3. in 4. at 5. on-in 6. with 7. of 8. for 9. in 10. over 11. for 12. by-by 13. with 14. in 15. By 16. by 17. in-with 18. into 19. on 20. of 21. for 22. to-of 23. to 24. for-with-to 25. between

PAGE 117

A. 2. That house was destroyed by fire. 3. The concert was enjoyed very much by the audience. 4. That book was taken from the desk by Bob. 5. The cake will be eaten by Walter. 6. The report has been finished by Beth. 7. The tickets will be left at the box office by Ms. Duke. 8. A box of flowers has just been left for you by the messenger. 9. The thief was easily captured by the police. 10. The lecture was attended by many people. 11. We were very much disappointed by the movie. 12. The export division is managed by Mr. Jones. 13. The money was returned by John last night.

B. 2. The fire destroyed the entire city. 3. The enemy captured the town. 4. Someone has stolen the money from my purse. 5. Mary found the book. 6. John has returned the book. 7. Many people all over the world read the book. 8. Paula delivers the mail.

PAGE 118

C. 2. A dancing class was started by them last week. 3. The accident was seen by Mr. Smith. 4. The report was left on the desk by him. 5. This film will soon be seen by everybody. 6. The report has just been finished by him. 7. The war was

followed by an economic crisis. 8. My briefcase has been taken by somebody. 9. Our written work was returned to us by the teacher. 10. Books are bought from that store by Valerie. 11. By noon the report had been finished by her. 12. The little boy was bitten by the mad dog. 13. The fog is blown away by the wind by midmorning. 14. You will be chosen by the committee as its representative. 15. The plate and the glass were broken by the maid. 16. The street was lined by tall trees. 17. The event was immediately reported by the newspapers. 18. The sound of music was heard by us. 19. Five suspects have been arrested by the police. 20. Our dog was played with by the neighborhood children. 21. He was ordered to take a long rest by the doctor. 22. The house was struck by lightning.

PAGE 119

2. It should be sent to us at once by them. 3. The mail is being delivered now by the mailman. 4. It has to be finished by him today. 5. He is being held for further questioning by the police. 6. A new group may be organized by them next week. 7. That letter ought to be written by you today. 8. The city is being defended bravely by the citizens. 9. The meeting cannot be held by them in that room. 10. The merchandise may be delivered by them while we are out. 11. The bill has to be paid by him before the first of the month. 12. The bill may be paid for us by him. 13. That question is being debated by Congress today. 14. For the time being, that group is being taught by Karen. 15. The plant ought to be watered by you once a week. 16. The merchandise is being shipped by the company today. 17. They must be warned by us of the danger.

PAGE 120

A-B. 2. This must not be finished-mustn't be finished-Must this be finished today? 3. The letter has not been sent yet-hasn't been sent yet-Has the letter been sent already (yet)? 4. The book was not published-wasn't published-Was the book published 5. The class is not taught-isn't taught-Is the class taught 6. The merchandise is not being sent-isn't being sent-Is the merchandise being sent 7. The thief has not been caught-hasn't been caught-Has the thief been caught 8. The fire was not started-wasn't started-Was the fire started 9. The chairs have not been put-haven't been put-Have the chairs been put 10. The jewels were not stolen-weren't stolen-Were the jewels stolen 11. The book will not be published-won't be published-Will the book be published 12. The lecture was not attended-wasn't attended-Was the lecture attended 13. The first prize was not won-wasn't won-Was the first prize won 14. The accident was not caused-wasn't caused-Was the accident caused 15. Our exercises will not be corrected-won't be corrected-Will our exercises be corrected 16. The house was not completely destroyed-wasn't completely destroyed-Was the house completely destroyed 17. The tickets have not been purchased-haven't been purchased-Have the tickets been purchased 18. The bridge was not designed-wasn't designed-Was the bridge designed

PAGE 121

C. 2. How was the building destroyed? 3. When will the merchandise be delivered? 4. Who had the money been stolen by? 5. Where was the child finally found? 6. What kind of accident was he injured in? 7. When is the mail delivered? 8. Who must sign the contract? 9. Where will the tickets be left? 10. When was San Francisco nearly destroyed by earthquake? 11. Where was the book published? 12. What was he operated on for? 13. Why was the boy punished? 14. Where was the note left? 15. When was the city captured by the enemy? 16. Where was the money put? 17. When will the bridge be finished? 18. Who was it designed by?

PAGE 122

2. was supposed to sail 3. was supposed to come 4. is supposed to be 5. is supposed to bring 6. was supposed to be written 7. was supposed to mail 8. is supposed to leave 9. was supposed to take 10. supposed to meet 11. is supposed to meet, is supposed to meet 12. supposed to write 13. am supposed to be 14. is supposed to take 15. is supposed to be published

PAGE 123

2. I never used to make 3. The accounting department used to be 4. Tom used to be a good employee and used to work hard. 5. I used to buy 6. This building used to be occupied 7. Betty used to have charge 8. Gary used to play 9. Laura used to go 10. He never used to do 11. He used to take 12. All meetings used to be held 13. Marcus used to be 14. I used to use 15. Mr. Earl used to work 16. I never used to catch cold. 17. It used to be my custom to practice (I used to practice)

PAGE 124

2. They would rather walk-They'd rather walk 3. We would rather spend the summer at home than in-We'd rather spend the summer at home than in 4. The doctor says that he would rather examine-The doctor says that he'd rather examine 5. I would rather not mention-I'd rather not mention 6. I would rather eat at home than in-I'd

rather eat at home than in 7. He would rather meet us-He'd rather meet us 8. I would rather speak-I'd rather speak 9. I would rather drive a small car than-I'd rather drive a small car than 10. Jean would rather study in this class than in 11. I would rather do-I'd rather do 12. He would rather live-He'd rather live 13. I would rather live-I'd rather live 14. I would rather work in my garden than play-I'd rather work in my garden than play 15. I would rather see a good movie than go-I'd rather see a good movie than go 16. He would rather attend; I would rather go-He'd rather attend; I'd rather go

PAGE 125

2. She had better rest-She'd better rest 3. Betty had better give 4. She had better not see-She'd better not see 5. They had better save-They'd better save 6. You had better not mention-You'd better not mention 7. You had better send-You'd better send 8. You had better not tell-You'd better not tell 9. You had better tell-You'd better tell 10. Neil had better prepare 11. You had better not drive-You'd better not drive 12. You had better not give-You'd better not give 13. You had better notify-You'd better notify 14. You had better spend-You'd better spend

PAGE 126

2. hasn't he? 3. isn't he? 4. doesn't she? 5. can't she? 6. didn't you? 7. isn't it? 8. wasn't it? 9. don't you? 10. don't they? 11. won't you? 12. haven't you? 13. aren't they? 14. doesn't it? 15. doesn't it? 16. aren't they? 17. didn't I? 18. wasn't she? 19. couldn't you?

PAGE 127

A. 2. have you? 3. will you? 4. is it? 5. was it? 6. did they? 7. did she? 8. was he? 9. does she? 10. will he? 11. does it? 12. did you? 13. have I? 14. is she? 15. have you? 16. can he? 17. should I? 18. will we? 19. would they?

PAGE 128

B. 2. isn't he? 3. has she? 4. isn't it? 5. don't you? 6. weren't you? 7. don't they? 8. do they? 9. doesn't it? 10. will we? 11. didn't you? 12. did you? 13. can't she? 14. does he? 15. isn't it? 16. doesn't it? 17. isn't she? 18. hasn't she? 19. isn't it? 20. isn't there? 21. didn't it? 22. didn't they? 23. won't you? 24. has it? 25. hasn't she?

PAGE 129

C-D-E. 2. doesn't she; wrote-didn't she; will write-won't she 3. isn't he; was-wasn't he; will be-won't he 4. doesn't he; made-didn't he; will make-won't he 5. doesn't he; spent-didn't he; will spend-won't he 6. doesn't he; came-didn't he; will come-won't he 7. isn't he; was-wasn't he; will be-won't he 8. aren't there; were-weren't there; will be-won't there 9. aren't they; were-weren't they; will be-won't they 10. don't they; watched-didn't they; will watch-won't they 11. don't you; enjoyed-didn't you; will enjoy-won't you 12. isn't it; was delivered-wasn't it; will be delivered-won't it 13. don't you; spent-didn't you; will spend-won't you 14. doesn't she; had to work-didn't she; will have to work-won't she 15. isn't he; was-wasn't he; will be-won't he 16. don't you; had-didn't you; will have-won't you 17. doesn't it; arrived-didn't it; will arrive-won't it 18. don't they; visited-didn't they; will visit-won't they 19. don't you; got-didn't you; will get-won't you 20. doesn't he; sat-didn't he; will sit-won't he 21. doesn't she; worked-didn't she; will work-won't she 22. isn't he; was-wasn't he; will be-won't he

PAGE 130

A. 2. There is 3. There is 4. It is 5. It is 6. It is 7. There is 8. There is 9. It is 10. It is 11. It is 12. It is 13. There is 14. There is 15. It is 16. There is 17. It is

PAGE 131

B. 2. There 3. It 4. It 5. There 6. It 7. It 8. There 9. It 10. It 11. There 12. It 13. It 14. There 15. It 16. It 17. There 18. It 19. There 20. It 21. There 22. It 23. It 24. There

PAGE 132

C. 2. It is important to learn new words every day. 3. It is very rewarding to study with Mr. Nathan. 4. It is foolish to pay so much money for a car that is old. 5. It is dangerous to drive so fast. 6. It is interesting to travel in foreign countries. 7. It is often helpful to be able to speak a foreign language. 8. It is unfair to blame Rocky for that mistake. 9. It is not interesting to study grammar for a lot of students. 10. It is important to understand grammar. 11. It is almost impossible for me to get up early in the morning. 12. It is faster to go by bus than by car. 13. It is not easy for a soprano to sing in such a low key. 14. It will be difficult to explain this matter to him. 15. It is foolish to work twelve hours a day at your age. 16. It will be pleasant to spend the afternoon at the beach. 17. It would be unwise to call her at this late hour. 18. It is not satisfying to eat quickly. 19. It is not easy to accept their apologies. 20. It is difficult to be comfortable in such hot weather. 21. It is not easy to compete for the top prize.

D. 2. There are a lot 3. There are two 4. There are several 5. There is a 6. There is a 7. There are a lot 8. There are two 9. There is a 10. There are two 11. There is only 12. There are two 13. There is a 14. There are several 15. There are a lot 16. There is a 17. There is an 18. There are curtains 19. There are a lot 20. There is a 21. There is a 22. There are two 23. There are some

PAGE 134

2. studying 3. going 4. waiting 5. buying 6. traveling 7. coming 8. listening 9. using 10. holding 11. receiving 12. painting 13. hitting 14. taking 15. going 16. making

PAGE 135

A. 2. swimming 3. spelling 4. calling 5. seeing 6. waiting 7. reading 8. visiting 9. finding 10. helping 11. attending 12. moving 13. helping 14. dancing 15. starting 16. leaving 17. seeing 18. seeing

PAGE 136

Answers will vary.

PAGE 137

A-B. 2. likes taking-likes to take 3. neglected telling-neglected to tell 4. prefer meeting-prefer to meet 5. start working-start to work 6. continue taking-continue to take 7. loves working-loves to work 8. prefers leaving-prefers to leave 9. hates leaving-hates to leave 10. start coming-start to come 11. likes studying-likes to study 12. prefers taking-prefers to take 13. begin increasing-begin to increase 14. continued building-continued to build 15. hates doing-hates to do

PAGE 138

2. will have seen 3. will have forgotten 4. will have died 5. will have been finished-will have been turned in 6. will have finished 7. will have been 8. will have forgotten 9. will have become 10. will have learned 11. will not have learned 12. will have been signed 13. will have learned 14. will have taken

PAGE 140

A. Answers may vary. 2. is teaching-is substituting 3. was working 4. are going to take 5. came 6. was coming-met-tried 7. have been 8. is ringing 9. had seen 10. have read (read) 11. will have completed 12. rang-was leaving 13. was shining 14. begins-ends 15. go 16. is knocking 17. has been heard 18. has studied (has been studying) 19. studied 20. is coming (will come)

B. 2. caught 3. is crossing 4. Does-walk 5. had left 6. will have visited (will be visiting) 7. will have been 8. had written 9. studies-see-is studying 10. will be doing-call 11. were you doing 12. has Harry been 13. was-has been 14. are you going to go (are you going) 15. had shot 16. was shining-had disappeared 17. began-ended-had lost

PAGE 141

C. Answers may vary. 2. tell-flatter 3. had lost 4. were driving-had 5. jumped 6. had come-gone 7. tripped-entered (was entering) 8. was chosen 9. has been seen 10. had taken 11. doesn't see-drives 12. hasn't danced-broke 13. went 14. did you go 15. will you go (are you going to go, are you going) 16. do you usually go 17. are you doing

PAGE 143

2. Sam has always been 3. He often goes 4. He seldom stays 5. We'll see you on Friday. 6. She played the piano last night. 7. at our home tonight 8. She has never spoken 9. Alice rarely asks for help. 10. Al is always late 11. He has always prepared 12. in the park on Sunday 13. We usually go 14. Do you ever go 15. I never go 16. that matter on Tuesday 17. an answer in the morning 18. Have you ever visited 19. Do you usually eat 20. Have you ever eaten 21. your exercises yet? 22. I have often spoken 23. Have you ever spoken 24. Has he always been 25. I have never been 26. that book twice 27. I have never read-Have you ever read 28. in college last week 29. He is often too busy 30. for Denver tomorrow 31. Does she sometimes forget 32. Does she generally get up 33. Has he always been 34. Nobody ever has 35. his work tomorrow 36. He rarely does his exercises carefully. 37. for California tomorrow 38. I met him there yesterday.

PAGE 145

2. He is now studying engineering at Columbia University. 3. He was so excited he couldn't think well. 4. The light was so bright that we had to cover our eyes from time to time. 5. She said that he had already had three operations. 6. I didn't even know that it was you who was calling me. 7. Throw me a kiss from the bus. 8. In a new skirt, Karen went to see the mayor. 9. Louise sometimes comes to our house for the lesson, and I sometimes go to hers. 10. I used to like the theater a lot, but now I go to the movies every night. 11. Of course I always speak German with my family and friends. 12. He is now studying

French as well as English. 13. He has been here two years; perhaps it is even more than that. 14. It was so cold that summer that we had to wear our overcoats now and then. 15. I have to write a lot of letters in English every day. 16. He said that he had already seen that movie. 17. He seldom comes to the lesson on time. 18. Simon gave me your message this morning. 19. Please read the whole sentence slowly. 20. We went to the theater last night.

PAGE 146

A. 2. still 3. still 4. still 5. anymore 6. anymore 7. anymore 8. anymore 9. still 10. still 11. still 12. anymore 13. still 14. still

B. 2. He isn't president of the club anymore. 3. They don't live on State Street anymore. 4. They don't visit each other regularly anymore. 5. He is not in love with her anymore. 6. They are not living in Quito anymore. 7. We don't see them at the club on Saturday night anymore. 8. It isn't raining anymore.

PAGE 148

A. 2. said the plane would probably get in 3. said he had to finish 4. said she'd get well 5. said everyone had to 6. said he had seen 7. said she had read 8. told her boyfriend she couldn't go 9. told me he'd finish 10. told him the lights weren't working 11. I told the waitress the bill was wrong. 12. said he was only 13. said he could meet 14. said she didn't do

PAGE 149

B. 2. said the students needed 3. told the teacher these exercises were difficult for them 4. said she didn't feel well 5. told me nobody could do that work as well as I 6. said he would be 7. told us she might be 8. said she had already seen 9. said he would see me 10. told us the baby was sleeping 11. said they didn't want 12. told me she had gotten my

PAGE 150

A. 2. asked me where I was going 3. asked whether (if) I was going to 4. asked whether (if) I had mailed . . . for her 5. asked me where I was going on my 6. asked her whether (if) she liked 7. asked me how I was 8. asked the salesclerk what the price . . . was 9. asked me when I would get back from my 10. asked her what time it was 11. asked when we would land 12. asked whether (if) it took longer 13. asked me what time it was 14. asked me how long I had studied

PAGE 151

B. 2. his name is 3. it is 4. she lives 5. my car cost 6. he put 7. we have 8. it is 9. he is 10. I was 11. she lives 12. she lived 13. she was 14. I had studied 15. he was 16. Helen is 17. I put 18. he lives 19. I would 20. I was 21. he could 22. I was

C. 2. He wants to know where Miss Dale went. 3. I wonder what time it is. 4. wants to know which file letter is in 5. like to know how much this costs 6. wants to know how he is 7. seems to know when he is 8. asked me when Mr. Saki would get 9. didn't know what the price . . . was 10. know where he is? 11. asked whether he had finished 12. ask him whether he lives 13. forget where I put it 14. asked him what it meant 15. know where she is going 16. tell me what time he was coming 17. any idea where it is 18. don't know whether she took 19. know how well she speaks 20. sure whether he is coming 21. tell anyone where he was going 22. don't know whether he returned

PAGE 153

A. 2. told us not to make 3. told me to try 4. begged us please to send 5. asked us please to sit 6. told me not to forget what she told me 7. asked us please to be . . . when we wrote our 8. told me angrily not to make

B. 2. The teacher told me to stay 3. The teacher told me not to make 4. The teacher told me to look . . . but not to open it. 5. The teacher told me to stop talking 6. The teacher told me to sit . . . in my seat. 7. The teacher told me to be quiet while she was talking. 8. The teacher told me to pay . . . what she said.

PAGE 154

A. 2. You should have gone 3. She ought to have prepared 4. You should have typed 5. You ought not to have said 6. We ought to have called 7. You should have visited 8. She ought to have been put 9. The package should have been sent 10. You should have spoken 11. They ought to have bought 12. He should have told 13. You should have paid 14. We should have gone 15. You ought to have put 16. You shouldn't have been

PAGE 155

B-C. Answers will vary.

PAGE 156

A. 2. She must have taken 3. They must have gone 4. Roy must have studied 5. She must have studied

6. You must have seen 7. The bank must have been robbed 8. He must have come

B. 2. They may have called 3. I may have left . . . I may have lost 4. They may have been 5. may have been stolen 6. The storm may have delayed

PAGE 157

C. Answers will vary.

D. 2. Professor Wiley may have learned Spanish in South America. I'm not sure. 3. Helen may have called while I was out. I'm not sure. 4. Mr. Reese may have been born in Europe. I'm not sure. 5. Mary and Helen may have had an argument. I'm not sure. 6. He may have passed all his exams. I'm not sure. 7. Grace may have gone shopping this afternoon. I'm not sure. 8. They may have been married in Seattle. I'm not sure. 9. It may have rained during the night. I'm not sure. 10. The New York Yankees may have won the World Series last year. I'm not sure.

PAGE 158

2. I'll go 3. I'll give 4. he'll get 5. we'll be 6. he'll find 7. he'll have 8. we'll go 9. I'll talk 10. I'll go 11. find 12. is. 13. turn 14. save 15. drive 16. calls 17. learns

PAGE 159

2. he would make, he'd make 3. we would take, we'd take 4. he would not feel, he wouldn't feel 5. he would have, he'd have 6. we would respect, we'd respect 7. I would read, I'd read 8. he would get, he'd get 9. If I owned 10. If she worked 11. If I knew how 12. he would make, he'd make 13. If he would not waste, If he wouldn't waste

PAGE 160

A. 2. If today were 3. If I were 4. If today were 5. If the weather were 6. If Pete were 7. If you were 8. I would feel 9. they would not be able to live 10. I would go 11. she would know 12. I would tell 13. I would live 14. he would try

PAGE 161

B-C. Answers will vary.

PAGE 162

A. 2. he would have been-he'd have been-he would've been 3. I would have come-I'd have come-I would've come 4. we would have gone-we'd have gone-we would've gone 5. you would not have caught-you'd not have caught-you wouldn't have caught 6. I would have written-I'd have written-I would've written 7. I would have gone-I'd have gone-I would've gone 8. I would have helped-I'd have helped-I would've helped 9. If I had known-If I'd known 10. If the weather had been 11. if I had known-if I'd known 12. if I had worn-if I'd worn 13. If he had studied-If he'd studied

PAGE 163

B-C. Answers will vary.

PAGE 164

2. is 3. go 4. get 5. get 6. invite 7. rises 8. call 9. rains 10. gets 11. arrives 12. do not arrive 13. see 14. sit 15. see

PAGE 165

A. 2. were 3. had gone 4. had 5. had had 6. were 7. lived 8. were 9. could 10. had studied

B. 2. I wish you would mail this letter right away, Kevin. 3. I wish you would be creative in your writing. 4. I wish you wouldn't make any mistakes. 5. I wish you would help me with this problem.

PAGE 166

A-B. 2. Bob did too-so did Bob 3. I am too-so am I 4. I will too-so will I 5. yours is too-so is yours 6. I did too-so did I 7. her brother is too-so is her brother 8. his wife has too-so has his wife 9. his assistant was too-so was his assistant 10. I did too-so did I 11. I did too-so did I 12. her sister will too-so will her sister 13. they do too-so do they 14. she can too-so can she 15. Cy has too-so has Cy

PAGE 168

A-B. 2. I didn't either-neither did I 3. her sister won't either-neither will her sister 4. I haven't either-neither have I 5. I hadn't either-neither had I 6. I wouldn't either-neither would I 7. I can't either-neither can I 8. I don't either-neither do I 9. mine isn't either-neither is mine 10. my wife doesn't either-neither does my wife 11. Mr. Barker wasn't either-neither was Mr. Barker 12. my friend couldn't either-neither could my friend 13. your son won't either-neither will your son 14. they don't either-neither do they

PAGE 169

A. 2. doesn't 3. can't 4. won't 5. did 6. don't 7. is 8. do 9. will 10. has 11. haven't 12. doesn't

13. doesn't 14. isn't 15. don't 16. I am not 17. do 18. don't 19. don't 20. I am not

B. 2. won't 3. will 4. does 5. is 6. are 7. has 8. did 9. isn't 10. can 11. can't 12. does 13. would 14. can 15. will 16. do 17. have 18. can 19. can't 20. don't 21. do

PAGE 171

A-B. 2. Isn't Conrad changing-Why isn't Conrad changing 3. Won't Helene be-Why won't Helene be 4. Won't she be-Why won't she be 5. Didn't Andrea take-Why didn't Andrea take 6. Doesn't Colleen like-Why doesn't Colleen like 7. Don't we like-Why don't we like 8. Aren't they going-Why aren't they going 9. Didn't Mr. Donahue bring-Why didn't Mr. Donahue bring 10. Isn't it-Why isn't it 11. Wasn't it-Why wasn't it 12. Hasn't it-Why hasn't it-13. Aren't the Starskys moving-Why aren't the Starskys moving

PAGE 172

2. Which month comes 3. What is 4. Who drove 5. What caused 6. Which umbrella belongs 7. Which notebook is 8. Which bus goes 9. Who lives 10. Which country is 11. Who is 12. What causes 13. Who has 14. What ocean is 15. Who won 16. Which book is 17. Who is 18. Who is doing

PAGE 173

A. 2. We'll have the oil changed-We'll get the oil changed 3. I should have the kitchen floor cleaned and waxed-I should get the kitchen floor cleaned and waxed 4. You had those letters typed-You got those letters typed 5. They had the oxygen level in their fish tank checked-They got the oxygen level in their fish tank checked 6. Phil is going to have his winter coat dry-cleaned-Phil is going to get his winter coat dry-cleaned 7. Did she have her computer repaired?-Did she get her computer repaired? 8. I should have the hole in my shoes repaired.-I should get the hole in my shoes repaired.

B. Answers will vary.

PAGE 174

2. What a beautiful day! 3. What a good-looking boy! 4. How well Gail plays golf! 5. How fluently they speak English! 6. How tall Pauline is! 7. How hot it is today! 8. What a hot day! 9. What good taste you have in clothes! 10. What a gorgeous car! 11. What a lucky card player! 12. What beautiful weather! 13. How old Penny looks! 14. What an interesting movie! 15. How wide the lake is! 16. How strange that behavior was!

PAGE 175

2. I did write 3. Ed did take 4. But we did study
5. I do want 6. I did do 7. Do call 8. she does live
9. he did call 10. he did reach 11. they did show
12. he does attend 13. I did have 14. Do bring
15. Do visit 16. does seem

PAGE 176

2. of (about) 3. in 4. to (with) 5. for 6. to 7. for
8. in (at) 9. in (at) 10. by 11. to 12. to 13. at
14. at (to) 15. in 16. from 17. at (about)

PAGE 177

A-B. 2. The man whom you were speaking to is
Dr. Evans.-The man you were speaking to is Dr.
Evans. 3. This is the room which they found the
clue in.-This is the room they found the clue in.
4. He is the kind of salesman whom it is difficult
to get away from.-He is the kind of salesman it is
difficult to get away from. 5. The person whom
you should speak to is Miss Williams.-The person
you should speak to is Miss Williams. 6. It is a
subject which we will never agree on.-It is a
subject we will never agree on. 7. The thing which
they were arguing about was really of little
importance.-The thing they were arguing about
was really of little importance. 8. It is a place
which you feel at home in.-It is a place you feel at
home in. 9. It was Bob whom we had to wait for
so long.-It was Bob we had to wait for so long.
10. It was Liz whom he borrowed the money
from.-It was Liz he borrowed the money from.
11. The room which we study in is on the second
floor. -The room we study in is on the second
floor. 12. This is the street which they live on.-
This is the street they live on. 13. I finally found
the book which I was looking for.-I finally found
the book I was looking for. 14. The students
whom she studies with are mainly from South
America.-The students she studies with are mainly
from South America. 15. The fellow whom I
roomed with was from Chicago.-The fellow I
roomed with was from Chicago.

PAGE 178

2. Roberta, the mechanic, repaired 3. cannot, of
course, reveal 4. Reese, the president of our class,
spent 5. not, in the first place, tell 6. Scranton,
Pennsylvania, on March 23, 1973, and 7. cannot,
after all, live 8. By the way, do 9. Marlene,
Henry's cousin, is . . . . Madison, Wisconsin.
10. you, Mr. Jones, on . . . . February 12, 2001?
11. Building, a famous landmark of the town, . . .
fact, it . . . February 12, Lincoln's 12. tennis,
swimming, and 13. Yesterday I met, quite by

accident, two former schoolmates, 14. day, June
20, 1998.

PAGE 180

2. (no commas) 3. (no commas) 4. Mary, . . .
hair, 5. hands, . . . tar, 6. (no commas) 7. (no
commas) 8. Pace, . . . story, 9. Wednesday, . . .
town, 10. Hemmingway, . . . business, . . . Glen
Acres, 11. (no commas) 12. hair, . . . morning,
13. (no commas) 14. (no commas) 15. Bridge,
. . . River,

PAGE 181

A. 2. (no punctuation needed) 3. mechanic, 4. (no
punctuation needed) 5. long time, 6. long time;
7. ambassadors, 8. go, 9. results, 10. cautious,
11. piano, 12. saxophone; 13. filthy, 14. time,
15. winter;

PAGE 182

B. 2. room, . . . around, . . . other, . . . then, . . .
enough, 3. Williams' store, . . . groceries, . . .
repainted; . . . consequence, 4. our new house,
which . . . famous architect, Mr. James
5. Harrisburg, Pennsylvania, to Albany, 6. (no
punctuation needed) 7. We, Ida, Ethel, and I . . .
going; 8. Ben Reese's brother, Tim Reese,
9. Saturday, January 16, 2003, . . . we had;
however, . . . day, Sunday, . . . to me; but, of
course, 10. climbed into the wagon; . . . out, . . .
country. It was lovely. 11. eleven, . . . meeting,
12. notified at once; yet, 13. Dr. Reynolds,
14. Commas, I noted, 15. Come here at once!
I need you immediately! 16. Did you see her
yesterday? Are you going to see her tomorrow?
17. When will we finish this exercise, Robert?

PAGE 184

2. make 3. advise 4. into 5. beats 6. spilled 7. stole
8. until 9. advice 10. poured 11. rob 12. in
13. make 14. does 15. win 16. advise-pour-spilling
17. stole-in 18. as far as

PAGE 186

2. am used to 3. too 4. very 5. less 6. besides 7. beside
8. left 9. no 10. not 11. not-not 12. forgets

PAGE 188

2. borrow-lend 3. Despite 4. lend 5. taught
6. despite the fact 7. have I seen 8. teach 9. learned
10. take 11. did the speaker mention 12. wait
13. could you find 14. foot-feet 15. In spite of the
fact 16. make 17. story 18. borrowing

INDEX